No Turning Back

Marion B. West

7916
Broadman Press
Nashville, Tennessee

Dewey Decimal Classification: 248.4
Subject heading: CHRISTIAN LIFE

Dedicated with love and gratitude
to the people in this book who have
allowed me to write about their
experiences—in hopes of helping
someone else when they feel like
turning back

All Scripture quotations, unless otherwise indicated, are from the
Revised Standard Version.

Scripture quotations marked "KJV" are from the King James Version.

Scripture quotations marked "TLB" are from *The Living Bible,
Paraphrased* (Wheaton: Tyndale House Publishers, 1971) and are used
by permission.

Library of Congress Catalog Card Number: 76-57508
Printed in the United States of America.

Introduction

"No turning back. What does it mean? Mama? Tell me what it means. Mama . . . Mama . . . ?"

I had already answered numerous questions that morning and I don't even like to talk before ten. I decided to ignore Jon.

"Mama, what does no turning back mean?"

I was about to give him a curt answer when suddenly I got excited wondering if a seven-year-old could understand what it did mean. I came into the den and saw him standing at my desk. He stared at the torn typewriter paper box that I had put the first rough chapters of this book in. On the top of the box I had penciled in NO TURNING BACK. I didn't feel like I could possibly write a second book.

I pulled up my desk chair so that I faced Jon. His face lit up knowing he was about to get real eyeball-to-eyeball conversation. His face anticipated whatever I had to say about his question.

"Jon, have you ever thought you should do something, but you were too scared or stubborn and you wanted to run and hide?"

"Yeah, lots of times."

"Grown people become scared and stubborn, too. They feel just like you and want to turn back."

We looked at each other silently as he let that soak in. He blinked his eyes rapidly, then grinned slowly. "Really?"

I nodded. "No turning back means going on when you don't feel like it, because there's someone who'll help you."

"Jesus," he said quickly, looking down at the words again and tracing the letters with his finger.

I looked at the words, too, and suddenly felt like NO TURNING BACK had been deeply carved into marble, instead of penciled on the top of a torn box, and I knew I had to keep working on it.

November 14, 1975

> I have decided to follow Jesus,
> No turning back, no turning back.
>
> Tho none go with me, I still will follow,
> No turning back, no turning back.
>
> My cross I'll carry till I see Jesus,
> No turning back, I'll follow him.[1]

Contents

PART ONE—HUSBANDS AND WIVES

Wives, fit in with your husbands' plans, for then if they refuse to listen when you talk to them about the Lord, they will be won by your respectful, pure behavior (1 Pet. 3:1, TLB).

1
But I Am Right, Lord

My husband's words hit me like a punch in the stomach. I had been on a spiritual mountaintop all day and oozed with love and appreciation for everyone. How was it possible that only one sentence from him could send me tumbling down into a valley? He didn't even look up from the paper he was reading. He had replied to something I said, and it wasn't the reply I had anticipated. It crushed me.

As the anger began mushrooming inside me, I thought, but I'm right, Lord. He's wrong. You know I'm right. He knows I'm right.

With grim determination I decided not to argue. (How spiritual can you get?)

I arose from my chair and stomped up the stairs, feeling Jerry's eyes on my back. I marched into our bedroom and slammed the door. Then, I kicked it. Throwing myself on the bed, I began complaining to God. "Did you hear what he said? He may not have meant it; probably didn't, but he said it! And he's wrong. I'm right. He's ruined my whole beautiful day. He doesn't know the suffering he's causing me. Do you see how I'm suffering? Oh, I'm so mad I'd like to throw something at him." I paused for breath.

The silent voice, that I really didn't want to hear, spoke to my heart. *It doesn't matter who's right.*

"Doesn't matter! Oh, yes it does! I'm right. He's wrong. And I'm hurting. He caused my suffering."

I can't help you with your present attitude.

I looked up at the ceiling, still fuming, and tried to decide if I really wanted to be helped. If it meant changing my attitude, I didn't think I did. I was right.

God seemed to wait on me to decide.

I sighed, resuming our conversation. "I don't feel like a Christian wife right now. I want to say all the mean things I'm smothering in my mind. I want to scream at him. He deserves it. I'm right!"

No answer.

"I am right, Lord."

I told you I can't help you if you insist on clinging to who's right.

"Well, I can't help how I feel."

Now, we're getting somewhere.

"You can help if I will allow you to?"

I can.

"OK, what do you want me to do? I'm about to explode. I have to do something."

Go back downstairs.

"Me go? Why can't you tell him to come up here? He drove me away. I've never gone back once I've left mad. And besides I am . . . ."

Don't say it again.

"I don't think I can go back down there."

Of course you can't. You'll have to depend upon me.

I sighed again. "Lord, will you help me get up off this bed and walk calmly down the stairs?"

Certainly.

I stood up, peeked in the mirror, and wiped the mascara from under my eyes where tears had left smudges.

As you walk down the stairs I will fill you with a love for your husband and cause you to forget his words as though they were never said. But first, you must give me your pride and hostility.

"I want that kind of love for him and I surrender, as much as I am capable, my pride and anger. But I'm still hurting, Lord."

Your husband is hurting, too.

"He is?"

Yes, and I want you to get your eyes off your suffering and consider his.

"But, Lord . . ."

Remember how my son hung on a cross in agony and looked down and was concerned about his mother's suffering. Now you be a little like him and stop thinking about yourself. Your husband is suffering. He just doesn't suffer as loud as you do.

"I never thought about that. He just keeps reading the paper."

He's hurting.

"I don't want him to hurt. What am I going to say when I get down there?"

Nothing.

"Nothing!"

Absolutely nothing. You talk too much. Sit and silently love your husband with the love I will supply for you.

I stood on the stairs for a moment, contemplating turning back. I laughed a bit, feeling foolish, trying to decide whether to go into the den and have a seat. Big deal!

"You're going with me, Lord?"

Of course. You'd never make it alone.

As I turned the corner in the kitchen, and started down the den steps, the sight of my husband sitting there reading the paper startled me. He didn't look any different, but I felt so different that my mouth opened in a surprised O. I quickly closed it, remembering the Lord had instructed me to keep my mouth shut.

I sat down and looked straight ahead at the television.

I felt Jerry look at me several times. I knew no expression of pain or suffering or bitterness was on my face. I felt too good inside. "Thank you, Lord. This isn't me."

A few moments passed. Jerry stood up and walked over to my chair and leaned down. He gathered me in his arms and held me as though we were young lovers and had been separated for a long time. Then he kissed me several times lightly, and held me again. We looked at each other and I don't think I've ever loved him quite as much as I did that moment. "Who cares who's right, Lord? Possibly I was wrong. But this isn't the time to say anything, is it? Just keep my mouth shut. This moment is very special."

Yes. Just keep quiet.

My heart pounded with gratitude. It seemed as though the powerful light of the sun had come out suddenly and radiated on an iceberg until it vanished. "Dear Lord, how many times have I missed this?"

You wouldn't believe how many.

"Thank you."

Jerry didn't sit back down but announced, as though nothing had happened between us, a change of attitude concerning something I had nagged him about for three and a half years. This had nothing to do with our original disagreement. It was an extra bonus. Nearly in shock, I thought, "This too, Lord? I can't believe it. Do you know how many times I've tried to convince my husband he needed to change his way of doing that? Why, we're having a miracle right here in our den on a Saturday evening in 1975!"

You have been obedient, and I love to reward my children for obedience, just as you do your children.

"Thank you, Lord. I've learned something, haven't I?"

Yes . . . finally.

"Lord, it doesn't matter at all who is right. But I would

have missed this if I had turned around and gone back
up those stairs. I guess I've turned back in a lot of situations when you were about to teach me something."

Yes, so many times.

"Thank you for being patient with me and for helping
me not to turn back tonight."

*You're welcome, dear child. Remember, obedience is
often difficult, but necessary and rewarding.*

"Lord, I believe I was wrong. I really do! How can
that be? I felt so sure I was right."

*Never mind. Don't even look back. That's the first step
to turning back.*

2
The Rain Experience

Without enthusiasm, I stood in line with my husband and three of our children to buy tickets to the high school football game. I could count the times I had attended a football game. I don't like screaming fans, hard seats or the complicated rough game, which I know nothing about. I've sat through an entire game and not known which team was "ours."

And tonight I was tired. "Go on without me," I had said nobly to my husband. I wanted to stay at home alone, leisurely clean up the kitchen, and then read. I wanted quietness. It had been a loud, demanding day.

"Please go," Jerry said. "I'll talk to you. I promise."

"Really?" I asked, surprised and pleased.

"Yeah, come on," he smiled at me.

Tired as I was, I laughed. It required skill to talk me into going to a football game. I did acknowledge to myself that I really wanted to see our daughter cheer. Julie had worked hard to become a cheerleader.

"OK," I gave in and went upstairs to change. "Remember, you promised to talk to me."

We had been seated only a few minutes when the tremendous claps of thunder began over the cheering fans. "It's going to rain," I announced, reaching up instinctively to touch my hair, which I had just had set.

"Look! Look! We've got the ball!" my husband elbowed me. "Look at 'em go."

"See the dark clouds gathering and feel the wind,"

15

I said fearfully.

"He's going all the way!" Jerry bellowed.

"I think I felt a drop," I raised my voice over the shouting fans around us.

"All right—let's go team!" Jerry screamed.

Well, I thought, we do seem to be talking, but this isn't exactly what I had in mind.

The cheerleaders shouted enthusiastically. I strained to see them, even though I didn't join in the exuberant cheering. Spotting Julie, I smiled proudly down at her, but she didn't see me.

Suddenly I screamed, "Look at the rain coming." Gazing up toward the lights I could see the falling mist becoming heavier.

I got up.

"Where are you going?" Jerry asked, eyes glued to the field.

"I'm not going to sit here and get drenched. This is ridiculous." So is football, I thought silently.

"I'm going to walk up to the refreshment stand so I can get under the shelter before the rain really starts. Anybody want to come with me?"

The children and Jerry refused.

By the time I reached the shelter others were crowding under and we stood packed, sardine fashion. The rain moved in suddenly with tremendous force so that the football field, players, and spectators seemed to disappear. Even under the protective shelter the wind blew the rain into my face.

The children are getting soaked—Jerry, too. And I remembered that cheerleaders continue cheering as long as the game goes on. Poor Julie!

Suddenly through the rain I saw Jerry running with Jennifer, Jon, and Jeremy, for shelter. I squeezed over as much as I could to make room for them. The others did, too. They ran under the shelter breathless, looking as though they had taken a shower with their clothes on.

"Dear Lord, whoever thought I would be doing this—at a football game of all places. I can't stand football. I don't belong here."

I looked down at our seven-year-old twins. They had worn new clothes and shoes. What a muddy mess. Thirteen-year-old Jennifer with rain dropping off her face and hair looked up at me hopefully—almost smiling. None of them complained. Jeremy shivered in the blowing wind. Jerry glanced out of the corner of his eye at me; then looked quickly toward the field.

"Lord, I give this impossible situation to you. I can't do anything about it. Please help us not to get sick, especially Julie. She's still out in it. I think my family is waiting on me to pitch a fit. Please help me accept this and not be a grouch."

As I prayed with my eyes open looking up at the rain, I felt unmistakable laughter welling up inside me and I laughed out loud, still looking up at the rain. I thought about opening my mouth and tasting it.

My family, as well as others, looked disapprovingly at me. I smothered my laughter, but the stubborn joy remained in my heart. "Lord, I accept this rain and mud—the entire situation; I'm glad I came. Thank you for this rain experience. Would you let it stop now so we can get on with the game. I really don't want to leave. I want to go back to the stands.

"Believe it's stopping," a man, standing by me, mumbled.

"Yep," another agreed.

I looked up. The rain did seem to be lighter. Soon it was only a drizzle. Jerry, our children, and most of the people left the shelter. I stood there a moment longer, marveling over my lack of anger or frustration. I couldn't seem to stop grinning.

Before I stepped out into the mud, I stooped and removed my shoes and rolled my pants to my knees. Then I sloshed out into the mud and felt it squish between my toes. My feet disappeared into the goo and I looked down in fascination, almost delight, like a child at play. I plodded back to the stands.

In a muddy area, Julie cheered with determination. Her new saddle oxfords were red with mud and it had splashed onto her new blue and white uniform we had just gotten from the dressmaker's. Her wet hair stuck to her face.

I climbed back up to my seat and sat down on a muddy, wet concrete stand without hesitation. Jerry and the children glanced over at me and their surprised looks melted into four similar grins.

"Thank you, Lord, that the rain stopped and that it's so warm tonight. Thank you, again, for this rain experience."

Julie looked up in the stands and when she saw that I had returned to the game instead of going back to the car to fume, she flashed me a tremendous smile as she continued to cheer. She cheered as though the stars were shining and her team was winning.

As the rhythmic cheering continued, I patted one bare muddy foot in time to the chanting and mused in amazement, maybe it's when we're willing to hang in there in situations we don't really want to be in that God gives us victory over them. How happy I was to be with my family, instead of sitting back in the car alone, fuming.

3
The Football and I

"I hate football," I muttered to an astonished friend.

"But surely you enjoy the atmosphere of the games," she insisted.

I shook my head firmly. No, I liked nothing about the games. At best, I amused myself by watching people in the stands, much to my husband's disapproval.

"Did you see that play?" Jerry often yelled excitedly, punching me in the ribs.

As usual, I had missed the play. I often attended games with him without seeing a single play. I couldn't even find the football most of the time.

Complaining in the heat and freezing in the cold, I continually questioned my husband Jerry like a patient in the dentist's chair, "Is it almost over?"

Once I asked Jerry if I could bring a book to a game I had promised to attend, but the look on his face squelched me.

Inevitably, the screaming fans made me jump, and I felt ridiculous and resentful because I was omitted from the excitement. When Jerry handed me the binoculars, I perpetually turned them toward the crowd, looking for someone I might know. Often Jerry carefully guided my field glasses back down to the game.

"Look at the field," he insisted. Sulking, I stared at what looked like a lot of ants scrambling over a bread crumb.

Once we attended a game with friends. Hilda refused

to sit with me. She knew I would attempt to talk about everything but football. No one wanted to sit by me. Finally, Jerry did. Feeling rejected, I watched the three of them jumping up and down and screaming and beating on one another. They spoke a language I didn't understand.

Televised games were worse. There weren't even the people in the crowd to watch. For years I begged Jerry to turn off just one game. I tried crying, pouting, and nagging; but Jerry watched the ball games. Still, he tried to get me to watch just one play with him.

"Look, look, look!" Jerry screamed at me one day, jumping to his feet and cheering at the top of his voice.

I retorted by jumping to my feet, "Read my book, read my book, read my book!" I was almost in tears.

Jerry didn't enjoy reading like I did, and he especially didn't enjoy my telling him what he should read. But he surprised me by saying seriously, "I will, if you'll watch this game."

Amazed, I quickly accepted his offer. I watched every play of a game between two unknown teams. He read my book, as he had agreed to do. He even said he liked the book.

My four children understood more about football than I did. Leaving a high school game one night, I wanted to say something "footbally." I was so happy the game was over that I decided to be pleasant.

"We really beat them, didn't we?" I announced proudly, looking at the 41-7 scoreboard.

"Mother," my children whispered, hoping no one had heard me, "we lost!"

About this time I attended a Bible study that focused on husband-wife relationships. We talked a lot about the responsibility of husbands and wives to each other.

Some friends who were attending the study teased me,

"Do you think God can help you like football, Marion?"

I flippantly replied, "Sure hope not!" But deep down, I considered the question seriously. Finally, I convinced myself that trying to please your husband doesn't mean football. It means things like cleaning out his sock drawer and keeping shirts ironed and maintaining neat garbage. (Certainly these were problems I could work on!)

Four years later I attended another study. For ten weeks I was taught once again how God created woman to be man's helpmate. The same Scripture I had heard years earlier was repeated. Much of it was already marked in my Bible.

The teacher carefully pointed out that wives shouldn't try to please their husbands through clenched teeth with a do-or-die attitude, but to call on Jesus for help.

I wanted to be a good wife, obeying happily. "But, surely, God doesn't expect me to like football . . . does he?"

Right then the teacher explained, "If your husband loves football and you don't understand the first thing about it, ask Jesus to help you." All my friends rolled their eyes my way. I pretended not to see them.

Driving home, I felt anger rising in me. I realized for the first time that I actually enjoyed hating football. I didn't want to give up my hate or my stubborn attitude.

"Jesus, I hate football so much," I prayed. "I don't know how not to hate it. You know I don't understand it, and I don't want to. Change my attitude. It's so ugly. Make me willing to go to a game cheerfully for Jerry's sake. And Jesus, show me something about a game that I can understand."

A few weeks later Jerry invited me to go to the Georgia-Georgia Tech game. They're the worst kind, I thought; but I smiled instantly and replied, "OK."

Jerry stood for a moment looking at me and grinning.

He reaffirmed the fact that we were going at least fifty times during the months that followed.

I began then praying for nice weather and that we would have a seat without the sun in our eyes. I asked that our four children would be able to stay with my parents. I asked Jesus to help me not fuss about the traffic or how far we had to walk, or complain about the overly enthusiastic and intoxicated people we probably would sit by.

The children's grandparents invited them to spend the entire weekend with them. I cheerfully canceled some Saturday plans that I had made. I even read a sports column in the *Atlanta Journal* the night before the game.

Jerry's mouth dropped open in disbelief when I told him about the column. He read the column and quizzed me on it. I passed!

The day of the game the temperature was 65 degrees, exceptional weather for December 1. Our seats were in the shade. Because of a crowd of sixty thousand, we were unable to get anything to eat before the game. We stood in line for almost an hour but had to leave without food. I didn't complain, even though my stomach did.

When Jerry handed me the binoculars, exclaiming, "Watch this play," I watched. I even found myself standing up when everyone else did in order to see. I couldn't scream like the lady behind me, or even cheer, but I watched most of the game.

I wondered if my friend Hilda was at the game and how surprised she would be if she could see me.

Occasionally, I felt Jerry's eyes on me as I watched the game. I even saw the ball a few times. I was aware that a man behind us had brought his bottle to the stadium, but I tried to ignore him and concentrate on the game.

Near the end of the game I heard a commotion a few rows behind us. The looks on the faces of the people in that section of the stands told me something tragic had happened. A doctor rushed up clutching his bag. Others scurried. Policemen hurried to the area.

Instantly, I spotted a woman frozen with horror. I remembered her. She and her husband had stood in line near us when we tried to get something to eat. They were holding hands and laughing and talking about the game. They were about our age.

The lady continued to stare at the people who worked frantically over her husband. They stopped working after a while, and attendants carried the man out on a stretcher. His wife followed mutely. After they left the stadium, I heard those who had sat by him talking.

"He was dead. They did everything humanly possible. It was just so quick."

I stared at the field again, but all I could see was the wife's crumbling face, pathetic and white under the wide-brimmed floppy hat. I remembered just a short while ago they had been laughing, talking, and holding hands. They had been together completely, in enthusiasm and shared interest. Now he was gone in an unexpected instant.

I still had a lot to learn about football, but I was allowed to learn an unforgettable lesson in life. I moved a little closer to my husband, grateful to be with him . . . even at a football game.

4
No More Black and Blue Fights

Through the years, I've slowly come to realize it's true what they say—opposites do attract and marry. I have to be on time, and Jerry never gets uptight about how fast the hands move around the clock. Sometimes I'm furious with him, and other times I envy him.

If we're driving to the store for a loaf of bread or going on vacation the time element gets to me. I stiffly sit in the car and fume silently. Sometimes I cry. I have blown the horn repeatedly, like a child. Then there's the silent treatment when Jerry finally arrives, pretending he's not late—that I'm early. A few times I've gotten out of the car and refused to go. (To the store, not on vacation.)

For seventeen years I've tried all sorts of psychological approaches, even pretending I didn't care about time. I've asked God to let me learn to be late. And I've tried—oh, how I've tried, but I just don't know how to be late. I can always feel my insides twisting into knots as the hands of the clock move with incredible speed. I end up ready ahead of time, pacing the floor muttering to myself.

One Sunday morning Jerry wrapped a towel around my head and wouldn't take it off till I hushed nagging about his being on time.

Even after I mastered the feat of keeping quiet (telling myself that I certainly was spiritual to accept my husband just as he was) I still seethed on the inside and Jerry could tell from the pained expression on my face that I was in agony, and we had a silent battle going once again.

Recently we were to attend a party across town—an hour's drive and the directions were complicated. We had never been there before. I figured we should leave at seven since the party started at eight. I was ready at ten till seven. The children had been fed, the kitchen cleaned. I redid my nails and checked my hair numerous times.

Jerry read the sports page. Finally he went upstairs and I heard water running.

So—we were going to be late again.

Mournfully, I sat on the carpeted steps, my favorite waiting place, and began my "ordeal." I had been looking forward to the party so much. It was a Christian gathering. Boy, we'll really fit in. By the time we get there, we won't be speaking.

As I sat with my chin in my hands I suddenly realized the familiar anger hadn't yet begun. Then a powerful thought reached me. *Why don't you praise me because you're going tonight?*

"Oh, I do thank you, Lord. I do."

Many husbands wouldn't be interested in this type of party. You have so much to be grateful for.

"Yes, I do. And I'm grateful."

Look at your watch, a different silent voice suggested.

I obeyed. Almost seven-thirty, I moaned. I felt the muscles in my neck tighten.

So what, the gentle voice encouraged me. *Don't listen to him. Satan always gets you uptight about being late. You've let him do it to you for years. Listen, you can have victory—tonight.*

"Thank you. I believe I will—somehow. Right now I don't even care about time. If we don't get there at

all, thank you because my husband wants to go to this
party tonight and he's upstairs getting ready. Now help
me keep meaning that, Lord. On my own, I'll take it
back. I can't do it by myself. You know how impatient
I am."

*You're going to have victory tonight because you finally
realize how helpless you are without me.*

For about twenty minutes I sat on the steps marveling
over the small miracle that was happening to me. I heard
Jerry moving about—faster, it seemed to me.

*Look at your watch now. You'll never make it. You're
going to be late again,* the other voice urged.

"Don't care," I insisted. I meant it. Joy bubbled up
inside me and time seemed to be standing still, just for
me. "Thank you, Lord," I whispered.

Just then Jerry hurried down the steps. "Hi," he said,
almost as though we were meeting for the first time.
We looked at each other silently for a few moments.
Then Jerry spoke. It wasn't so much what he said, as
the look he gave me. Suddenly, I realized I'd been starved
for that look many times—and didn't know what I wanted.
It's a very special look that every wife knows.

"You didn't say a word," he beamed.

"I know! I know!" I squealed happily.

As he drove the car, we both grinned silently, like
children. Then I noticed that Jerry wore the new socks
I'd bought him some time ago. I'd laid them out tonight,
hoping he'd wear them. "Oh, you're wearing the new
blue socks I bought you. They're nice."

"Yeah, they are nice. Just wish you'd gotten blue instead
of black."

"They are blue," I said with determination.

"No, Mannie—they're black."

"Silly, they're blue. You never could tell blue from
black."

"Guess you can't either. You always mate a blue with a black."

"Well those are brand-new and they're blue."

"Marion, I know black socks when I see them."

"Why in the world would I buy black socks? You don't need black socks!"

"I was wondering that myself."

"The manager of the men's department assured me they are blue."

"Well, you and the manager are wrong. They're black."

"Bluuuuuuueeeeee," I screamed.

Jerry pulled off the road, stopped the car, stuck one foot up to the level of the steering wheel and together we hunched over his foot, glaring at the sock.

"What color is that?" he bellowed.

Before I could scream blue again, the gentle voice spoke to my heart. *He's doing it to you again. Satan doesn't want you two to go to this party. And certainly not as happy as you were. You've given him a defeat (after eighteen years). Does it really matter to you what color the socks are?*

I sat back, relaxed, giggled a little and said softly, "Maybe they are black, after all?"

Jerry looked at me quickly. He put his foot back down and grinned, "Well, they sure look black. I like 'em. They're nice socks." He cranked the car and we continued.

"Lord, of course it didn't matter. But that's what most of our arguments are about—little things. I would never argue with Jerry about a big decision like buying a new car or moving. I would do whatever he said—but blue socks seemed such a little thing. Oh, Lord, you must have stood by so many times wanting to help us so we wouldn't fight and turn away from each other."

5
There Are a Lot of Ways to
Say You Are Sorry

Looking at the clock for the umpteenth time I calculated that my husband was now an hour-and-a-half late for supper. I had fed the children and myself. The kitchen was a mess and his plate at the table didn't look too inviting.

I knew he had had a lot of work to do today as well as for the past few weeks. He said his work should lighten up in a few more weeks. But I had been pretty patient, I thought. Greeting him warmly each night, even when he worked sixteen hours; sitting with him while he ate; keeping quiet because I knew he was too tired to talk; not bothering him with my daily problems. I had even asked the children not to engulf their father with math problems and financial needs, or to share their victories of the day with him until after he had eaten.

But I had had the flu the week before, gotten out of bed in two and a half days, and hadn't popped back to my old "happy homemaker and helpmate self." I dragged through each day and couldn't seem to get caught up.

Tonight, supper was a tremendous effort that I thought I couldn't get through. It was as though a ball and chain were attached to me. My teenage daughter helped some. One of the seven-year-old twins spilled his milk and I cried silently as he smeared it around on the floor with a dry towel.

Feeding everyone was finally over once more. Everyone, that is except my husband. Somehow I couldn't face the kitchen that looked like a battleground. It had been a nice dinner—two hours ago. Jerry could have called and said he would be late again. I got up from the table, leaving the four children sitting there finishing up, and escaped to the living room sofa. I lay on the sofa, thinking, I'm not a short order cook. I shouldn't be expected to plop hot meals on the table at a moment's notice. Feeling terribly sorry for myself, my anger toward my husband flourished.

It felt so good to lie down. I drifted off to sleep into a world without crumbs or responsibilities.

I heard Jerry open the door. *Get up,* part of me urged—*greet him.*

Big deal, an ugly side of me insisted. *Stay put.*

I was tired and angry by now. Rest felt wonderful. If I kept my eyes shut I would be back asleep in that neat, orderly world in a moment.

"I'm home," Jerry announced.

"Lo," I mumbled.

"What kind of greeting is that for a husband who has worked all day for you and the children. You wouldn't believe my day."

"Ummmm."

"Where's my supper?"

"In the kitchen—of all places."

"Is it cold?"

"Speck so."

Julie, our thirteen-year-old daughter and peacemaker, piped up, "I'm heating it, Daddy."

A pang of guilt shot through me, but the ugly part of me said, "Good for her. She needs to learn to do things around the house."

I drifted back to sleep while Jerry ate alone. I vaguely heard Julie and Jennifer doing the dishes. It didn't take much effort to allow myself to go deeper into sleep. I've been sick, that troublemaking part of me rationalized. This was not my usual behavior, and a small part of me kept shouting, get up. Make things right. But the stubborn nature won and I went soundly to sleep. I awoke to find my husband standing over me, speaking in an unfriendly voice.

"What's wrong with you?"

"Tired and sleepy."

"Well, get up, can't you?"

"No."

Maybe I would have, but out of the corner of my eye I saw a briefcase bulging with work. That settled it! I got up, eyes half shut, and stumbled upstairs to bed.

"Where are you going?"

"Bed."

"At 8:30?"

"Yep."

"Come sit with me." The angry tone remained in his voice.

"And watch you work?" I went to bed.

Julie tiptoed into my room and suggested, "Mama, why don't you go sit with daddy?"

Guilt shot through me once again, but I sighed, feeling helpless to respond to that part of me that still cried out to make things right again. I drifted to sleep.

The next morning Jerry was gone when I woke up. I barely remembered him kissing me good-bye. I felt wonderfully rested, but not so wonderful about my actions. All day, thoughts seemed to follow me around.

You must say you were wrong and that you're sorry. You have to do something. I remembered we had been married for twelve years before I had ever said the words, "I'm sorry. Forgive me. I was wrong." For three days I had tried and couldn't get the words out. It was one of the hardest things I had ever done. I can still remember the look on Jerry's face and exactly where we were standing in the house when I apologized. His face sort of lit up, then melted into a fantastic grin, like it did the first time he looked at one of our newborn babies. He accepted my apology instantly and insisted much of the problem had been his attitude.

Over the next six years I had said that I was sorry more often and with less difficulty. Now the time had come again. I knew God was urging me to apologize to my husband.

"I'm going to do it, Lord. I have to do it." But God seemed to keep saying something else to me. Finally, I thought I understood him. *There're a lot of ways to say you're sorry.*

Maybe this wasn't a time for just words, as important as they were. Something else—but what? As soon as I opened my mind to the "but what?" ideas flooded my brain. First: Put a sign on the door that says something like "Welcome Home Husband."

Second: Cook a super-special supper (even if he's late again).

Third: Wax the kitchen floor.

"Wax the kitchen floor," I nearly shouted. I have a cute little sign that hangs in my kitchen. It says, "I don't do floors or windows—the housekeeper." It's more than a decoration. It's my declaration. But I began to daydream about waxing the floor.

Fourth: Wear something that's not "house clothes."

I couldn't make up my mind to do any of it. Suppose I did all this and Jerry came home late again. Wouldn't my sign look ridiculous? Suppose his supper got cold again? Suppose someone spilled milk on my waxed floor?

As the afternoon wore on I developed a big burst of energy and began waxing the floor. The children tiptoed around me and oohed and aahed. Julie got down on her hands and knees for a closer look and said, "Beautiful, Mom."

Excited about the floor I went to extra trouble in preparing supper. About 5:15 I ran upstairs and put on white slacks that I usually wear out and a "good top." I worked on my hair, put on lipstick, curled my eyelashes, and dotted on my favorite perfume. Julie walked by and grinned silently at me. She gave me an "I approve" signal by making a quick circle with her thumb and forefinger. Might as well go all the way, I thought happily. I made the sign. It said, "Welcome Home—Husband, Father, and Breadwinner!" Then I drew a stick figure wife leaning on her broom and clapping her heels together for joy. Flowers bordered the sign.

Supper was about done and in my enthusiasm I realized I had gotten it ready thirty minutes early. Just then I heard a car door slam and ran to the window. I gasped aloud. My husband was home early! I heard his steps, then a pause at the door. He opened it laughing, kissed me, and handed me a box of chocolate covered peanuts, my favorite.

"You're early," I squealed.

"Yeah. I just decided to come on home for a change."

He looked down at the floor. The children all said, "Mama did it, Daddy."

"Nice," he nodded.

After supper as I munched my peanuts, I thought how marvelous God's timing is. When he speaks to one of his children about an apology, he often prepares the heart of the one to receive it. Or better still—leads both to say, "I'm sorry."

Neither of us had said the words this time. God had suggested something much better and we learned there are a lot of ways to say you're sorry.

6
Letting Go

Letting go hasn't come easy for me.

Friends have told me, "Well, I've just turned this or that over to God. It's in his hands, now." They always made it sound so simple and smile victoriously. I've often wanted to ask, "But, wasn't it hard? How long did it take? How do you really let go of someone or something?"

For me, it has remained one of the most complicated steps of faith a Christian can attempt. No one ever told me exactly how to do it—they just assured me that releasing people and things to God was a must.

I've managed to give God a problem, even a person, for awhile—but inevitably, I reach out and grab on again. Letting go, I decided, must be the ultimate in faith.

How do you, I pondered, really give someone or something to God?

I've assured myself time and time again, "There, now. I've given that to God. Good for me."

But deep in my heart, clammy little hands of fear reached out and clutched desperately in a paralyzing grip the someone or something I wanted to let go of—trust God with.

Recently my mother-in-law and father-in-law took three of our children for five days. Our fourth child was in the hospital and I needed to be with her. During those days I experienced a keen awareness that I wasn't responsible for the other children. My responsibility centered around the hospitalized child. I loved the children who were with their grandparents, prayed for them, missed them. But they were not my responsibility for five days. I didn't doubt for a moment that someone who loved them was meeting all their needs.

Looking out the hospital window at the sun coming up, I thought, this must be what it's like to let someone else take over. In a sense, I've given my children to their grandparents for five days.

Then I reasoned, if I really gave someone to God, it would be sort of like this—only permanent.

Just as my in-laws hadn't demanded, "Give us the children. You can't possibly care for them now," neither would my heavenly Father demand that I give someone or something to him. But if I chose to do so, he would gladly receive the person or thing that I surrendered fully to him.

Often, when I'm having great difficulty learning, God gives me an amazingly simple mental picture. He reduces great truths to their simplest forms for me. He gave me one of these illustrations concerning how to let go.

In my mind I saw a child standing at the edge of a pond. She held tightly onto a string to which was attached her prized possession—a beautiful boat. She ran up and down the bank of the pond pulling her boat where she wanted it to go.

One day her father suggested that she let go of the string and see what the boat could do without her dragging it around.

"Oh, no," the child cried. "I can take the boat everywhere. I can even run all the way around the pond with my boat. I'll never let it go. I love it too much."

The patient father encouraged his child bit by bit. "Let go. See what will happen. Let the waves and the wind have their way with your boat. You've held on to it for so long now."

One day the child finally opened her small fist and watched the string quickly disappear into the water. Then she looked in amazement at her little boat. It didn't sink or turn over. It bobbed out into the very deepest water. Her boat rode the waves gallantly. It went much futher than the child could have taken it.

The little girl sat down on the bank and quietly marveled. Then she wondered why she hadn't let go sooner. Eagerly she encouraged other children, "Let go of your boats! Let them go." But the children only held on tighter. They didn't understand at all.

As I imagined that picture, my heavenly Father urged, "Open your hand and heart, child. Just let go. You've held on for so long now." Then ever so gently he reminded me, *I know what letting go of someone you love is like—I know—but it's necessary.*

And somehow, with his help, I let go of my husband in that moment of time, April 12, 1976, for always. It was our eighteenth wedding anniversary. I even opened my hand and imagined a string sliding quietly out of my grasp. As I did this, I experienced an exhilerating sensation of release so that my sudden tears of joy fell onto my open palm.

I'd really let go after years of struggling and pretending. Since then I've let go of other people and things. I often have to actually open my hand and see that string mentally sliding out into the choppy waters. Sometimes I close my eyes and visualize my boat moving out, seemingly alone. And when I'm tempted to reach out into the water and grab onto the floating string, even for a moment, I imagine myself backing away from it and saying, "You be in charge, Lord. Do whatever you will. I don't know much about boats." Then I see the wind pulling my little boat away from the shore and I stand helplessly on the bank, watching, waiting—expecting.

PART TWO—CHILDREN

Children are a gift from God (Ps. 127:3, TLB).

7

The Bluehorse Tablet of Love

From upstairs I heard the unmistakable thud of something being spilled on the kitchen floor. Running down the steps, I saw seven-year-old Jon standing there holding an almost empty soft drink bottle. Most of the sticky drink was spilled on the floor. I assaulted him verbally for spilling the drink, which he wasn't allowed to have with his breakfast anyway.

His twin brother, Jeremy, ate his cereal silently. Jon wailed, "It wasn't my fault. Jeremy . . ." That's when I really lost my temper. Nothing had ever been Jon's fault!

After cleaning up the mess I sat him down to a bowl of cereal. Embarrassed, probably not wanting me to know how sorry he was about the spilled drink, he laughed and clowned around as he began eating. Pow! The bowl sloshed across the table onto the kitchen floor and into the hall leaving behind a trail of milk, sugar, and cereal. Some of it even turned the corner and spilled up the stairs. Only Jon could manage that!

A rage began in me that I couldn't control. I screamed and slapped out at him. Trying to dodge my hand he pulled away and overturned his chair and fell into the mess he had made. Completely exasperated, I cleaned up the cereal remembering that before his daddy had gone to work he had spanked Jon for fighting with his brother and for whining. That made me angrier and I continued to tell him how clumsy he was and would always be.

He watched silently, standing perfectly still, as I cleaned up the cereal. I had to pick up each piece separately. I knew I should insist that Jon do it, but in my anger I didn't even want him to have the satisfaction of repairing the damage. "There's still a bowl of sugar on the table and more milk. Why don't you pour that on the floor, too?"

As Jon and Jeremy went out the door to wait for the bus, I cautioned Jon, "If I see you starting any trouble outside, you'll come back inside. No roughhouse. Stand still. Trouble just happens around you."

The boys hadn't been at the stop three minutes when I peeked out to check on Jon. I don't know what provoked it, but he was hammering Jeremy on the head with his fist, like one of the Three Stooges. I opened the door and yelled for him to come inside. When he reached the steps, I jerked him through the door and pushed him against the wall. "Why—why, do you have to make trouble all the time?"

He started crying and said, "I don't have a tablet for school. You got the wrong kind yesterday and I have to have one today."

Like adding coals to a fire, his just now telling me this compounded my fury. "Dummy, you don't even need a tablet. You would lose it. Stand at the window and look at the other children behaving." I pushed him away from me forcing his face against the window.

"I'm hot in this raincoat. 'Lemme take it off."

"No. Just stand still." I can't remember all I said, but I remember that the words felt bitter and hot coming out of my mouth and I couldn't seem to stop them. Then I saw the bus turning the corner and opened the door and pushed Jon outside, as he screamed back at me, "I have to have a tablet." There was open terror on his face. After I shut the door, it seemed to me he was really saying, "I have to have love." And I knew I couldn't honestly give him the love he wanted right then.

He climbed onto the bus with the rest of the children and if I had been a man I probably would have pounded the front door with my fist. Instead, I sat down at the kitchen table with a cup of coffee and a pounding heart.

Washing my cup in the sink I thought, I'm a Christian—a Christian mother. How can this be happening to me? I don't deserve God's forgiveness and I can't even ask for it.

Gently, God spoke to my heart, *You must ask. I can't forgive you until you ask.*

"I can't. I can't. I don't deserve forgiveness."

What you deserve doesn't count. Ask.

I tried, but couldn't. Even in the silence of my heart, I couldn't form the words—Lord, forgive me.

I'd planned to meet an out-of-town friend for lunch. She had been my Sunday School teacher in another town. I had looked forward to today. Now, I didn't even want to get dressed. It would be so long until the boys were home from school, and I could make it up to Jon somehow. What kind of day would he have now? What chance did he have with the send-off he had gotten this morning?

Then I felt the icy indifference and pride around my heart melt into a great pool of need and I cried out, "Oh, Lord, forgive me. Please forgive me, even though I don't deserve it. I ask your forgiveness and I need your help."

You have it. Ask Jon's forgiveness.

"I will when he comes home."

No, go to the school, now.

"Get him out of class?"

Yes, hurry.

"But, Lord . . ."

It's the only way.

"I don't know . . ."

But by then it was as if a magnet drew me to the school. Dressing quickly, I smiled, imagining Jon's surprised face when he saw me there. As I ran out to the car another thought plunged into my mind. "Why don't you take him the Bluehorse writing tablet?"

I will! I will! That's a wonderful idea.

I drove up to the school with the tablet and practically ran inside. The secretary was out of the office for a moment so the principal called Jon over the intercom, "Jon West, come to the office now, please."

Oh, dear, I thought. Jon would think he was in trouble again and the principal was going to accuse him of something. I waited for him anxiously. Then I saw him coming before he saw me. Unmistakable fear in his eyes, he walked—defeatedly, chewing on one lip; but he came quickly to whatever awaited him.

Love for him so filled my heart and overflowed that I blinked the tears away and prayed, "Thank you, Lord, for helping me come. How close I came to not coming." Jon's eyes traveled quickly from my face to the Bluehorse tablet and then his face exploded into an understanding grin.

"Mama, you brought me the tablet! Thanks."

I knelt down to his level and gave it to him and of all the ridiculous things—my tears plopped right down on the tablet for Jon to see. He looked up at me silently for a moment, and I couldn't say all the wonderful things I had planned, so I just said, "I'm sorry. I was wrong. I love you."

"That's OK, Mama."

I knew the unwritten rule that forbids asking for a kiss from a seven-year-old in front of people. And I knew the principal and other office workers were right behind us. Students roamed the halls. "Would you give me a kiss?" I whispered.

He reached up and gave me not only a kiss but a tremendous bear hug, so that I nearly fell onto the floor. Then he turned with the Bluehorse tablet tucked under his arm and headed back for class. There was an unmistakable bounce of security in his walk.

That afternoon Jon handed me his school papers. I took them expecting the usual large amount of incorrect math problems circled in red. *100!* Big red letters. And the teacher had written, "Jon really tried today and did beautiful work. I'm so proud of him!"

8
Teaching on a Bike

Looking back now, I know there must have been times in my mother's life when she could have easily turned back. She lost two children before I was born. My father died when I was two. Jobs for women were scarce in 1938, but my mother obtained one at the local bank. She worked her way from a beginning bookkeeping job to assistant vice-president in the thirty-eight years of employment with the Granite City Bank. She never said or implied, "See how I'm going on even though it's hard. See me struggle." Instead I grew up watching a lovely woman who with quiet determination and dependence upon God moved forward. For the most part, I never guessed the going ever got rough. I just assumed that my mother loved to get up before day and rush through the housework, cook me a good breakfast, and then get me off to school. We didn't have a car. She walked to work, regardless of the weather. Then, she walked home for lunch to save money; walked back to work; then walked home late in the afternoon. In the winter it was already dark when she got home. In the summer I can recall sitting out by the streetlight in front of our house on Myrtle Street and watching for her to turn the corner. I would run up the hill to meet her. Running up that hill was a wonderful experience, even as a child I thought, "This is special. Someday I want to write about this."

It didn't occur to me then that she might have enjoyed more adult conversation instead of my constant chattering. She listened intently to my happenings of the day, smiling, nodding, asking questions, gasping in open amazement.

I knew nothing of complaining mothers. I had seen my mother with double pneumonia and a raging fever calmly tell our family doctor, "I'm not going to the hospital on Christmas Eve. I'll be fine. You'll see." She was, too.

I did realize that many of my friends' mothers had a lot more leisure time and I wished my mother and I could have had more. But, I decided it wasn't the quantity of time spent with someone you loved, but the quality. Only, I didn't know those words then. But, I figured that out early in life and felt good about it.

I never thought much about our not having a car except on rare sunny days when I longed to go somewhere on an adventure. My mother had the answer for that. We hiked to a special spot in a nearby woods called "Sleepy Hollow." It became another world for us. Sometimes my friends went with us and they marveled that my mother liked to do such fun things.

Wednesdays and Sundays were always the days we had together. On Sunday, I knew that we would go to church, have roast beef for dinner and then read the paper. But, you never could tell about Wednesday. I remember one Wednesday so vividly I can almost become a child again as I relive it. I had no idea I was being taught anything. There was no lecture involved and it was fun.

I was seven years old on that hot day in July of 1943, when my mother and I went visiting on my yellow bike. I sat behind Mama, holding onto the seat and remembering to stick out my feet so they wouldn't get caught in the spokes. When we came to a hill my mother got off and pushed. "Want me to get off, Mama?"

"No, sit tight, Mannie. You don't weigh enough to

matter." The sun was hot on our backs—so hot I thought perhaps my mother would turn around and forget all about our visit, but she didn't.

"Does Janie know we're coming?"

"No, she'll be surprised."

That made the visit even more exciting. I could hardly wait to see Janie again. She had come to take care of me right after my daddy died while my mother worked. I had never been to Janie's house. In fact, I had never been over to the Negro section of town very much. It was a long way. Sometimes I rode with my friends when their mothers drove their maids home. I loved to go with them. The children over there always seemed to be having so much fun. And the families were large. I didn't have any sisters or brothers. My neighborhood was very quiet. I like to hear the uninhibited laughter that came from the Blue Moon Cafe. It made me smile to myself.

Mama pedaled across the railroad tracks and the pavement ended abruptly. The red Georgia dust floated up like powder and I gritted it between my teeth and watched it rapidly cover my white sandals. Crossing the tracks I was afraid that the gift might bounce out of the bicycle basket. I peeked around Mama to be sure it was still there. It was a pretty package, wrapped in pink and blue paper. I could hardly wait for Janie to open it. She hadn't been to work in a long time. Mama had told me that Janie was going to have a baby and couldn't work. So I stayed by myself sometimes, or with a neighbor and felt pretty grown-up, but I missed Janie. Mama reminded me before we left the house not to ask Janie about her husband—because she didn't have one. I nodded and didn't ask the next question that popped into my mind.

Some brown-skinned children in faded shorts stopped playing hopscotch and came to the edge of their dirt

yard and looked silently at us—two strangers on a yellow
bike. Mama waved first, then I did. Instantly all the
children waved back to us at the same time, grinning.
They waved till we were out of sight. A brown woman
sweeping her walk called out to us, "Afternoon." The
brown mailman nodded to us. I decided I liked being
on the bike better than in a car. You could see a lot
more—right into people's faces. But I thought, it's just
like turning a page in my coloring book and finding that
someone had colored all the people brown.

Finally we stopped in front of a small, unpainted house
that seemed to lean a bit to the left. The red-dirt yard
was swept clean. Great, big pretty zinnias surrounded
the little house and more than made up for its lack of
paint and crooked angle. The flowers looked sweetly
familiar to me. Janie used to bring us armfuls.

Janie's mama sat on the front porch in a straight back
chair, shelling peas. She hopped up when she saw us and
spilled some of the peas. She ran down the steps like
we were somebody from out-of-town. She was tall and
skinny with long arms and big hands, wild gray hair, and
a rasping voice that I liked. She threw her long arms
around Mama, then hugged me. "You 'don rode that
bicycle all de way over here to see Janie."

"And the baby," I added. "We brought him a gift."
I grabbed the gift from the basket and blew the dust
off.

Inside the house we found Janie in an iron bed. Red
zinnias in a fruit jar sat on a table close to the bed. I
had never seen Janie lying down before. She looked
different. Smaller. Her white gown made her seem even
browner—like coffee. Then I saw the tiny baby in the
crook of Janie's arm. She held him just the way she used
to hold my doll when we played house. For a moment
I felt like I was going to cry, but I didn't. I grinned

instead, but wondered, why isn't Janie smiling? She doesn't look glad to see us. What's wrong? Why is she turning her face to the wall?

I sat carefully on the bed and very gently touched the tiny baby's hand. He gripped my finger just as tightly as a grown person. Tears welled up in my eyes and I bent down to kiss him. "Oh, Janie! You sure had yourself a fine baby boy."

Janie looked at me then. There were tears in her eyes. They rolled down her face and onto her neck. She didn't wipe them away. I had never seen her cry before.

Mama reached down and touched the baby and asked, "How are you, Janie?"

She didn't answer Mama.

Mama said, "The baby's beautiful."

Janie still didn't speak. She just kept looking at the wall. Mama went around to the other side of the bed and started talking to Janie in a soft voice. Janie's mama went back to the front porch. I was so busy looking at the baby and touching him that I didn't hear what Mama said, but pretty soon Janie was smiling again. Then she sat up in bed and opened the gift. She looked at it for a little bit and then lifted the blue gown out of the box and sort of rubbed it against her cheek. She noticed the printed tag that was still attached to the gown. She bit the string into and began reading slowly. Her lips moved when she read. Janie put the tag into a drawer and put the gown on the baby. She let me turn the sleeves back and pull his little hands out. "I'm going to call him Billy. You like that, Mannie?"

I nodded furiously, still holding his hand. Pretty soon we had to leave. Janie's Mama walked out to the bicycle with us and kept saying, "Thank you."

In about two weeks Mama told me that Janie was coming back to take care of me. At first, Janie's Mama kept Billy, but then Janie brought him some days. We had wonderful times together. I pretended he was my little brother and when he got older I taught him to sing songs, jump rope, and to count. I even pushed him around on my bike. I coaxed him to eat vegetables like Janie had done for me. Long after Billy could walk, I would stick out one skinny hip, plop him on it, and carry him around. He would wrap his legs around me and hold on real good.

Right after Janie came back to work, Mama said I could ask about Billy's daddy if I wanted to—that he and Janie were married. I nodded like I understood.

On rainy days we stayed inside and colored while Janie ironed and sang church songs to us.

Billy and I sat together on the floor, our heads bent over a coloring book and I taught him to color the people on every page brown and pink.

9
A Touch of Honesty

"I'm sick, Mama. Come get me."

The tone of my fifteen-year-old daughter's voice kept me from taking the time to ask questions. "Be right there." I hung up the phone and left immediately for the school.

Julie sat on the curb outside the school building. She got up slowly when she saw me and walked toward the car. I noticed right away that she moved in an unusual way, holding her head in an odd position. I opened the car door for her. As soon as she sat down I noticed the tiny beads of perspiration standing out on her pale face. Her hands shook. "I may throw up," she said in a strained voice, looking straight ahead.

"What's wrong?"

"Something's wrong with my shoulder and neck—I can't move them," she answered, still unable to turn her head to look at me.

As I drove, Julie screamed when I applied the brakes suddenly, and her head pitched forward. "Don't do that again, please." I slowed down and tried to avoid sudden stops; but still she cried out when I turned curves. At home she got out of the car cautiously, holding her head perfectly still. There was no way I could help her except by opening the door. Inside the house, she headed for the living room sofa instead of her bedroom, upstairs. As she tried to lie down, she moaned. While I phoned the doctor, I heard her cry out again.

The doctor couldn't see her until 5:15. We had a five

hour wait. I went into the living room to tell her. She still sat up. "I can't lie down, help me. I can't use my neck muscles at all. When can he see me? Can we go right away?"

I put my hand under her head. The more it hurt, the more frightened she became and the pain seemed to intensify. She appeared caught in a vicious circle of pain. "When can the doctor see me?"

"Not till five."

Tears filled her eyes and she blinked them away.

What was I waiting for? Why didn't I offer to pray with her? Could it be that she might refuse my offer with a, "Oh, Mother . . ." sigh. Still mulling my decision I brought the heating pad and two aspirins. Suppose I offered to pray and she said yes; how would I pray? Simply ask God to make her well right there on the sofa? What a tremendous prayer that would be! What faith! Suppose he didn't heal her—then what? How would it affect her faith? Deep in my heart I couldn't decide to ask for something I didn't believe was really going to happen. And quite honestly, I didn't believe God would heal her right then and there. "I wish someone were here with enough faith to ask God to heal Julie."

Jo Ann popped into my mind. We often prayed together and she seemed to be able to pray for healings as simply as a child praying, "God, make the rain go away." Often when I read about the faith that moved mountains, I thought about Jo Ann. We lived near Stone Mountain and I could imagine someone saying to Jo Ann, "We're going to ask God to move Stone Mountain. Will you pray with us?" In my mind Jo Ann always answers softly, "All right. Where do we want to ask him to move it."

But Jo Ann wasn't here. Neither were any of my other friends, with whom I often prayed. Suddenly I blurted out, "May I pray with you, Julie?"

"Yes," she answered quickly. Kneeling beside her, with my hand under her head, I thought, but I still don't know how I'm going to pray, Lord. "Will you help me pray?"

He seemed to respond, *What can you believe?*

I thought for a moment and answered in my heart, "That you can stop this pain somehow. Through sleep! Lord, I believe you can put Julie to sleep right now. I believe that." Julie and I shut our eyes and I prayed aloud, "Thank you, Lord, that I was here when Julie's call came. Thank you for helping me pray. Thank you for answered prayer. Father, please let Julie go to sleep right now—let her sleep deeply and soundly, unable to feel any pain until we get to the doctor. Thank you. In Jesus' name, Amen."

I opened my eyes and watched Julie. Her eyes remained closed and her breathing deepened. I slipped my hand from underneath her neck. I knew she was asleep, but I said her name. "Julie." Then louder, "Julie." She didn't respond.

"Oh, thank you, Lord, for helping me pray. Thank you for not letting me resort to a "bless-and-keep-and-help" kind of prayer. Thank you for this blessed sleep. I know it's from you."

Just then the doorbell rang and I glanced back at Julie. She didn't move. I answered the door and my mouth fell open. There stood Jo Ann. We saw each other often at church, school, shopping, and in prayer groups, but we almost never visited.

"You came!" I clapped my hands, and she backed away a bit and looked behind me. Then she laughed softly, "Was I supposed to?"

"Yes, of course. Come in."

"I left the car motor running. I just stopped by for a moment to see if you wanted to ride somewhere with me." After she came in, I explained about Julie and how

I had wished for her to be here to pray with me. We went down into the den to pray. We thanked God that Julie slept. Then Jo Ann asked God to heal Julie. I knew he would. Julie's deep sleep and Jo Ann arriving to pray with me increased my faith so that I too asked God to heal Julie.

Julie woke up two hours later, after Jo Ann had gone. "Mama, I'm hungry." Julie is small, but can eat like two men. I started to the living room to tell her I would bring her a tray, but she was up and walking into the kitchen. I watched her silently. "Can I have tomato soup and a sandwich and Sprite?"

I fixed it. Julie looked normal, except very sleepy. She ate with her eyes closed. "Can't stay awake," she mumbled. She wolfed down the food, then without mentioning her neck, went up the steps to her bedroom. I guided her because she was so sleepy she seemed to have been drugged. She tumbled onto her bed and curled up in her favorite sleeping position.

While she slept, I went about my housework with a special kind of joy—closely kin to that same happiness I had known when getting a screaming baby to sleep. While vacuuming I thought about my prayer. And I realized with new clarity that God knows the prayers of our hearts before they are ever uttered from our lips. How many dishonest prayers had I prayed, perhaps trying to impress people or even God? And how many times had I turned away from the great privilege of prayer because I feared to ask for "too much"?

I awakened Julie at quarter of five. She stretched, smiled, got up, and brushed her hair. "That sure was a good sleep." I noticed all her movements. She tried to look over both shoulders. She couldn't quite do it, but came close.

We were both thinking the same thing. This trip to

the doctor isn't really necessary. But we went, anyway. He said he could feel where Julie's muscles had been pulled. He added, "This could be a lot worse. I've seen people who couldn't move."

She shot me a quick half grin that said, "I know, Mother. Prayer is powerful, but thanks for not going into details right now with the doctor."

I smiled back at her, reassuringly. I had spoken to this doctor on other visits about my beliefs concerning God's healing. I didn't feel prompted to say any more today.

Driving home I resolved not to turn away from prayer because I didn't know how to pray. God had demonstrated to me that he would help me pray honestly if I asked for his help.

10
Second Chance

Thirteen-year-old Jennifer looked frightened as she marched her seven-year-old brothers to me. Tears welled up in their eyes. I sensed something was terribly wrong.

Jennifer spoke softly, "Mama, the boys want to tell you something." Jon and Jeremy hung their heads and stared at the floor without speaking. Jennifer spoke again, "They were striking matches under your bed. Lots of matches. Burning paper, too. And they lit a candle. Jon singed his hair and Jeremy burned his finger."

Never would I have thought my children would do this. I had lectured them about fire and its danger. So had Jerry. I had even told them if they ever found matches to bring them to me and I would give them a quarter. I had read too many heartbreaking accounts of what playing with matches could cause. Gratitude moved in my heart, crowding the guilt, and I breathed a prayer of thanksgiving. They hadn't been hurt this time. It must never happen again.

"Why did you do it?" I demanded. They shrugged their shoulders. Quickly I ran upstairs to be sure no fire smothered. I got sick to my stomach when I saw all the old Christmas boxes and tissue paper I had stored under my bed. After the initial shock wore off I became angry. I spanked the boys and put them in separate rooms to remain there until I told them they could come out. Periodically, I stormed into one room, then the other, and lectured to them again about fire. They listened silently without protesting or blaming the other, but I didn't see any remorse. Oh, they had been afraid of the spanking they knew was coming and cried when they got it. But once that was over, they appeared almost nonchalant—smug.

Back downstairs vacuuming, I thought, they mustn't just think this behavior today falls into the category with other mischief. I have to do something to make a lasting impression on them. As I vacuumed I imagined flames engulfing the bedspread, then the boxes under my bed. I saw firemen bending over the bodies of my boys—our home destroyed—small caskets. I kept the pictures clearly in my mind to prevent my rationalizing, boys will be boys.

Nearly an hour later they called to me, "Can we come down?"

"No," I answered back. Then I reasoned, well, what am I going to do? Keep them up there indefinitely? "Lord, what am I going to do? Please show me what to do. They don't realize what fire can do. Help me."

An idea began growing in my mind. I pushed it away several times. Surely what I thought about was too drastic for such little boys.

By the time I finished vacuuming the downstairs I felt convinced I knew what to do. I would turn them in to the arson department at the fire station.

No, I can't do that, a part of me argued. Firemen and people in the arson department are busy. Besides they'll think I'm some kind of a nut. They may even think Jon and Jeremy are firebugs.

"Lord, is this what you want?"

I felt it was, but I thought, what if someone says when I call, "Hang up lady. Your children are your problem. Get off the line."

Then I argued, but suppose someone will listen to me

and help me. Still confused, but feeling I must make the call, I looked up the number and dialed the phone.

"Yes ma'am. May I help you?" a friendly voice asked.

I told him my problem and he quickly said, "You need to speak to Captain Griffith. He's not in, but I'll have him call you right away." Then he added the words I desperately needed to hear, "Lady, if more mothers would do what you're doing, we would never know how many little lives we could save each year. Thank you for calling."

I told the boys not to go off, that a Captain Griffith of the fire department would be calling soon and we would probably go and see him.

"Why?" Jeremy bellowed.

"I'm going to tell him what you boys did."

"What—what will they do to us?" Jon wailed.

"I don't know. I've never turned in anyone before for nearly setting a fire."

Jon's mouth fell open and Jeremy's mouth turned down as he tried not to cry. "Will, will he put us in—jail?" Jeremy asked.

"I don't know. We'll see."

Every time the phone rang they came running to see if it was the Captain. When he did return my call the boys were standing by the phone. The Captain asked me to bring them right to the station. He also asked their ages and then asked permission to show them a picture of a burned child. I assured him it was fine with me.

As Captain Griffith began speaking to them I saw that they were almost trembling. I could see tears in the corner of Jon's eyes. I had never seen my boys sit so still. He spoke as only a man can who has pulled lifeless bodies from fires and witnessed pain beyond description. He told Jon and Jeremy about a little five-year-old boy who had been playing with fire and candles. Some kerosene blew up and stuck to the child's skin. All the way to the hospital the child had screamed, "Am I going to die?"

Captain Griffith had assured him that he would be all right. But two days later he attended the little boy's funeral. "When I looked down in that little casket at that little fellow with a baby Bible and his teddy bear, I'm not ashamed to tell you, boys—I cried," he said hoarsely, remembering the child.

A tear slid down Jon's face. He didn't wipe it away.

"You know what we do to people who set fires on purpose?" he asked sternly.

Jon and Jeremy shook their heads.

"We put them in jail."

Silence.

"You're too little to put in jail, but if this happens again, we could put your daddy in jail. He's responsible for you."

More silence.

"Your mother ever tell you not to play with matches?"

"Yes, sir," they whispered.

"Speak up. I can't hear you."

"Yes, sir," they nearly shouted, suddenly sitting erect.

"Didn't listen, did you?"

"No, sir," they responded, loud and clear.

"Look here," he opened a book. "Pretty little girl isn't she?"

"Yes, sir," they said in unison, leaning forward, almost smiling.

He turned the page and I felt hot tears brimming my eyes. The child no longer human except for her curly hair. The smile on my boys' faces vanished quickly. They stared at the picture, not even daring to look at me for comfort.

"She played with matches," Captain Griffith said.

The lecture continued for about twenty minutes, with

more illustrations and questions. Finally, the Captain said, "If there's ever a next time, I won't just talk to you."

They nodded silently.

"Thank you, Lord, for this powerful idea and for helping me have the courage to go through with it."

Captain Griffith stood up. My boys did too, still looking at him gravely. He stuck out his hand and spoke in an amazingly gentle voice. His eyes softened. I'm not sure it wasn't tears that softened them, "I'm your friend, fellows. The graveyards are full of little boys and girls like you who thought it was fun to play with matches. They didn't get a second chance. You did."

"Yes sir," they smiled at him in open admiration, as though he might have been Bat Man, and pumped his hand long and hard.

All the way home the boys were silent except for Jon's single comment, "He's nice, ain't he, Mama?"

Now everytime we drive by the fire station one of the boys exclaims, "Hey, that's where that nice Captain Griffith works." They glance back until the station is out of sight.

11
Learning to Listen

It appeared that Jeremy had a one-track mind. Nearly every time he said something, it centered around a poster contest at school.

I had been out of town all week at the *Guideposts* workshop. I had won—finally, and the trip to New York had been everything I had dreamed about for five years. I felt pretty important as I stepped off the jet back in Atlanta. My family waited for me and after we had embraced, I started telling them about my trip. At least I tried to. Everyone wanted to tell me something—especially eight-year-old Jeremy. He jumped up and down in order to be heard and his voice carried above the other children's, and even Jerry's.

Everyone needs something from me. They don't want to hear about my trip. What is it Jeremy keeps saying?

"Poster paper, Mama! I have to have poster paper. We're having a contest at school."

I put him off, promising we would talk about it later. Back at home I readjusted to the telephone, doorbell, sorting laundry, driving in the car pool, answering questions, wiping up spills, and fighting off the creeping knowledge that no matter how hard I tried, I couldn't keep up with the needs of my family. As I moved about hurriedly, trying to decide what must be done next, I began to know what to expect. Jeremy inevitably appeared to remind me, "I need the poster paper, Mama."

Gradually though, he spoke more softly, almost as

though he talked to himself. So I put Jeremy's request at the bottom of my long list of things to do. Maybe he will just hush about the poster paper, I thought hopefully.

On my third day at home, I managed to salvage about fifteen minutes to try to type on an article. Sitting at the typewriter, I heard the dryer stop. Another load of clothes should be put in. Two important phone calls needed to be returned. One of my daughters had pleaded with me several times to listen to her recite part of *The Canterbury Tales*. For over an hour one of the cats had meowed right in my face trying to get me to feed her. Someone had spilled orange Kool-aid on the kitchen floor and smeared it around with a dry towel. It was past time to start supper and I hadn't even eaten lunch. Nevertheless, I typed joyfully for a few delicious minutes.

A small shadow fell across what I typed. I knew who it was before I looked up. I glanced up anyway. Jeremy stood quietly watching me. "Oh, Lord, please don't let him say it again. I know he needs poster paper. I need to type." I smiled weakly at Jeremy and kept typing. He watched for a few more minutes, then turned and walked away. I almost didn't hear his comment. "Contest is over tomorrow, anyway."

I wanted to write so much that with a little effort I could have tuned out his remark. But I couldn't ignore the silent voice that spoke urgently to my heart. "Get him that paper—now!" I shut off my electric typewriter. "Let's go get the paper, Jeremy." He stopped, turned around and looked at me without even smiling or speaking—almost as though he hadn't heard.

"Come on," I urged, grabbing my purse and the car keys.

He still didn't move. "Do you have something else you have to get?"

"No, just your poster paper." I headed for the door.

He lagged behind and asked, "You're going to the store—just for me?" I stopped and looked down at him. Really looked at him. Spots of whatever he had eaten for lunch at school stained his shirt. Untied, flopping shoes and traces of orange Kool-aid that turned up at the corners of his small, grim mouth, gave Jeremy a clown-like appearance.

Suddenly, a look of utter delight shot across his face, erasing the disbelief. I don't think I'll ever forget that moment. He moved with amazing speed, and running to the bottom of the stairs he threw his head back and shouted, "Hey, Julie, Jen, Jon, Mama's taking me to the store! Anybody need anything?"

No one answered him, but he didn't seem to notice. He sprinted out to the car still wearing the Christmas morning expression. At the store, instead of running in ahead of me, he grabbed my hand and started rapidly telling me about the poster contest.

"It's about fire prevention. The teacher announced it a long time ago, and when I first told you, you said we would see later. Then you went out of town. The contest ends tomorrow. I'll have to work hard. What if I win?" He went on with endless enthusiasm as though he had only asked me one time for the paper.

Jeremy didn't want an apology from me. It would have spoiled the joy. So I just listened. I listened to him as intently as I ever have listened to anyone in my life. After he bought the poster paper, I asked, "Do you need anything else?"

"Do you have enough money?" he whispered.

I smiled at him, suddenly feeling very rich, "Yes, today I just happen to have lots of money. What do you need?"

"Can I have my own glue and some construction paper?"

We got the other items and at the cashier's, Jeremy, who usually doesn't confide in strangers, said, "I'm making a poster. My mama brought me to the store to buy the stuff." He tried to sound matter-of-fact, but his face gave him away.

He worked silently and with great determination on the poster all afternoon.

The winner of the contest was announced over the school intercom two days later. Jeremy won. His poster was then entered in the county competition. He won that too. The principal wrote him a letter and enclosed a check for five dollars.

Jeremy wrote a story about the poster contest. He left it lying on his dresser and I read it. One sentence jumped out at me. "And then my mama stopped typing and listened to me and took just me to the store."

And a few weeks later a large yellow envelope came in the mail addressed to Jeremy. He tore into it and read aloud slowly and almost in disbelief the Certificate of Award. "This certifies that Jeremy West has the distinction of reaching the state finals in the 1976 Georgia Fire Prevention Theme and Poster Contest." It was signed by the comptroller general of Georgia, Johnnie Caldwell.

Jeremy fell on the floor and did somersaults, laughing aloud. We framed his certificate and often when I see it I remember that almost—almost I turned away from his request to get him some poster paper.

PART THREE—FRIENDSHIP

A true friend is always loyal, and a brother is born to help in time of need (Prov. 17:17, TLB).

12
A Little Bit of Light

"Dear Lord," I prayed wearily, "please don't let the phone ring again. I have just a few minutes to get the boys ready for church." Exhausted from nearly two hours of sympathizing with a disillusioned new Christian over the phone, I walked out of the kitchen.

Ring-g-g, the telephone shrilled at me. "No!" I wailed aloud, but answered with a normal, "Hello."

"Hullo," the childlike voice on the other end said quickly. "How are you tudday?"

Tears welled up. I was too tired to talk with Agnes. I prayed silently, "Why Lord? Why did she have to call now? I'm in a hurry and too tired to listen. She wants something. She always wants something. I don't feel like giving right now."

"Hello, Agnes," I said between clenched teeth, feeling the muscles in the back of my neck tighten.

If she noticed the unfriendly tone in my voice, she chose to ignore it.

"How you been?" Agnes asked.

"Fine," I said stiffly, "and you?"

"Oh, dust fine," she rambled on and I stopped making an effort to understand her. Her severe speech impediment made it imperative that I concentrate continuously to understand her. She was easier to follow in person, when I could watch the movement of her mouth.

I first met Agnes when my church group visited a home for destitute women. I noticed Agnes immediately, and was drawn to her childlike quality, though her personal appearance was far from attractive. We soon became friends.

She would visit our church when someone would drive her in from the mission. One evening, during an evangelistic meeting, Agnes was the only person to go forward on the hymn of invitation. The following week she was baptized. I've heard since that Agnes has made many such professions of faith.

So what? I had thought, in defense of Agnes. God's love can reach anyone, even if it takes a little longer with Agnes. I will not judge her.

But I was disappointed that Agnes' character hadn't changed since I had known her. For over a year I had responded to her phone calls, listening, and visiting her until she moved out of the mission.

Her call came when I was in my most uncaring mood. It wasn't convenient to be her friend now. I was tired. The clock ticked away precious minutes as my mind rushed ahead calculating all the things I had to do.

Call Jon and Jeremy inside, bathe them, find clean clothes, take Jennifer to choir, and call Julie and remind her of the time, insisting that she hurry home. And where was my husband? I would have to round him up, too. Besides all that, we were taking guests to church with us. I didn't want to be late picking them up.

Agnes talked on and I realized she was asking the same question over and over.

"Tan ooh hep me?"

"What do you need, Agnes?" I asked.

"Oh, tank ooh. I need yell-oh tirt wast."

"A what?"

"A yell-oh tirt wast," she repeated slower.

"Dear God, I prayed, what is she saying?"

"I don't understand, Agnes."

"I haf new yell-oh pants. Need yell-oh tirt wast to go wif dem."

"Oh, a yellow shirtwaist."

Again I prayed, "God, I don't care if she needs a yellow shirtwaist. I just don't care this time. Why couldn't she call at another time when I felt charitable?"

Tears of frustration welled up and I blinked them away. I had so much to do for my family, and I already felt drained. I wanted to be halfway pleasant when we picked up our friends for church. Now here was Agnes asking me for a yellow shirtwaist.

She held the phone patiently. I could hear her breathing. Agnes has more patience than anyone I've ever known, and I suddenly envied her.

"I don't know where you live, Agnes."

"I gif ooh directions."

With my sense of direction and Agnes' instructions, I knew that wouldn't work.

"Maybe I could mail you something." I said, still looking at the clock and thinking in the back of my mind, she won't know her address.

"O-tay. I get address. You wait."

I waited and waited, watching the clock as more time slipped by.

Finally she was back and calling out numbers, slowly, like a bingo announcer. What she said didn't make sense.

"That's your telephone number, Agnes!"

"Dat's right. Ooh write it down on paper."

For nearly five minutes she tried to call out the numbers in their correct order. Finally, I had something that looked like it might be a telephone number. "Now the address, Agnes. Tell me your address." For another five minutes I wrote down what she called out, ending up with *Pklndeen* Street.

"Agnes, let me see what I can do about the shirtwaist.

I'll mail it to you if I can get your address, okay?"

"O-tay. You send me tirt-wast. Tank ooh. Bye."

I hung up the phone and ran to the front door, calling the boys and my husband, wondering how we could get to church on time. In the back of my mind, I told God, "I can't possibly get her address. You know that. I'll have to forget about the blouse for Agnes."

"But what if you could get the address?" I thought as if God were asking.

Exasperated, I muttered, "Then I'll send the shirtwaist!"

Thoughts of Agnes waiting for the blouse crossed my mind for the next few days, but because of a hectic schedule of appointments and duties, I had to concern myself with other things.

Then, talking with a new friend on the phone, I casually mentioned Agnes by name to illustrate a point. Sarah was silent for a moment, then asked, "Are you talking about Agnes Morgan?"

Surprised, I stammered, "You know her?"

"Don't you remember? I mentioned that a friend called me to come get her out of jail recently?"

"Yes," I answered, quickly.

"Well, it was Agnes!"

"You know Agnes," I whispered almost in disbelief. Over a million people in this city and Sarah just happens to know Agnes!

There was unmistakable joy in her voice, "Yes, oh yes, I know Agnes. God is teaching me how to love her, just as she is. Marion, when you and I look at Agnes, we don't especially like what we see. She seems—beneath us."

"Yes, she does, Lord. I can't help it. She does."

Sarah continued, "Well, have you ever thought that when God looked at you and me in our sin, we must have looked just like Agnes looks to us? But God loved us still! Just as we are—with unconditional love."

I couldn't say anything.

Sarah continued speaking softly, "God's teaching me, through Agnes, about loving and accepting people just as they are. Be grateful for Agnes. It's really no great Christian accomplishment to love someone you like. But Agnes, well, I praise God every day for sending her my way."

Finally, I spoke, "Do you happen to have her address?"

"Sure do."

The next day I joyfully mailed two blouses with a short note to Agnes. I realized, as I dropped the package off at the post office, that getting a shirtwaist blouse for Agnes wasn't an everyday mundane incident, but a chance to shed a tiny bit of light which God had sent my way.

13
The Peppermint Miracle

Wistfully, I decorated the tall tree. I had so hoped we would be in our new house by Christmas. I had hated the cramped, weather-beaten rental house from the moment Jerry drove up the narrow driveway and announced, "Here it is." The backyard was deep in mud that rainy March day we moved in.

"Where's the grass?" three-year-old Julie asked as Jerry carried her through the mud. I held Jennifer, not yet one, in my arms.

"We'll have grass at our new house," I answered. And I thought bravely, as I fought back tears, maybe there'll be neighbors here I'll enjoy and children for the girls to play with

Soon I discovered eight children lived next door to us, but they were painfully shy and any move toward being friendly sent them running into their house.

I almost never saw their mother. Mrs. Long worked each day. Our houses were so close together we shared a driveway, but an invisible wall kept us from being neighbors. I called to her sometimes, but she seemed too tired or busy to notice me. Maybe she was embarrassed about her husband's loud, arguing manner that she knew I could hear.

Julie and Jennifer were excited about the tree and helped me decorate it. It was one of our loveliest trees, reaching almost to the high ceiling. Its cedar aroma stirred many nostalgic memories for me. The music from the record player sounded like Christmas. Packages waited underneath the tree. Jerry had been whistling "Jingle Bells" for days. My small kitchen was loaded with good food I planned to cook when our families joined us for this special day. Cards from friends that I had read and reread were on the coffee table.

But I felt dark and lonely inside.

This sad feeling will go away. Surely it will. I just miss my old friends and neighborhood. Last Christmas it seemed the doorbell or the phone rang constantly.

Oh, that wonderful moment of opening the door to find a neighbor standing there with a sample of goodies from her kitchen or a small, homemade article gaily wrapped.

I missed a neighbor running over to borrow a cup of sugar or a bit of nutmeg, and the friends that called out to me when I went to the mailbox.

I tried to look forward to spring when we would be in our new house, but it seemed a lifetime away. I wanted to feel the way you were supposed to feel on Christmas.

As I put away boxes that the decorations had been stored in, I fought to keep back the tears. How could I explain to Jerry what was missing? Maybe tomorrow, Christmas Eve, the special feeling would come.

The next day the girls and I wrapped some last minute gifts. As I cooked supper I told them about what Christmas was like when I was a little girl. Even reliving those happy memories didn't fill the vacuum inside me.

Finally, it was time for Jerry to come home. We sat at the window looking for him. It was dark and cold outside. A light drizzle fell. I turned on the porch light and wondered if anyone noticed our door decorations. I felt like we were on a desert island.

"Look, Mama," Julie exlaimed, "Mrs. Long's coming to see us."

I looked, expecting to see her checking her mailbox or perhaps walking to the grocery store that was near us. She and some of her children usually walked and pulled their groceries home in a buggy. But she was coming toward our house. She held her face down to avoid the icy rain.

We moved back from the window and sat on the sofa waiting for the sound of the old doorbell. I answered it on the first hint of a ring.

She wore a wool scarf and clutched her coat tightly about her throat. Little drops of rain clung to her dark hair. Her breath circled about her face. She held something in her hand.

"Come in, come in, Mrs. Long," I said.

"Hello," Julie said warmly, and Jennifer reached up and held onto her coat.

"Here, let me take your coat. Do you think it'll snow? Please sit down."

But she held her coat even tighter and replied, "No, no, I'll keep it on. I just wanted to bring you this." She handed me a bowl covered in tinfoil. A little red bow sat on the top. I opened it to find small broken pieces of peppermint candy filled the bowl.

"Ohhh, we love peppermint. Thank you so much. It really isn't Christmas without peppermint, is it?" I popped a piece in my mouth and gave the children a piece. When I offered Mrs. Long some, she declined.

"I work in the candy factory, you know. I can pick up the broken pieces anytime I want to. I just wanted to come over and say 'Merry Christmas.' "

"Thank you, thank you. Please sit down for just a moment." She hesitated a bit, then sat down, loosening her coat. She smiled down at Julie and Jennifer who sat as close to her as they could get. I noticed the tired lines beneath her warm smile.

She told the children, "Your door certainly is pretty. We've been admiring it."

"You have?" Julie beamed at her, then me.

We began talking about our children and Christmas. She told me she had two days off for Christmas. Then she insisted she had to leave.

"Oh, your bowl, Mrs. Long. Let me empty your bowl."

"No, you can bring it back sometime. And bring your little girls when you come."

"All right. We'll be over soon. Wait just a minute, will you?"

I ran to the kitchen, as she chatted with Julie and Jennifer, and cut most of a fruitcake, arranging the pieces on a colorful Christmas plate. Quickly, I wrapped it in clear wrap and covered it in Christmas stickers. I rushed back to the living room and gave her the cake. "Merry Christmas, Mrs. Long."

She took the cake, "Why, thank you."

As we watched her go back into the dark night, I thought, how easily she could have pushed aside that idea of coming to my house and bringing us a gift of peppermint candy. "Thank you, God, for sending her."

I looked at the small bowl of peppermint candy. It didn't look like so great a gift. But, instantly, I remembered another gift that had been given quietly and humbly on Christmas Eve nearly two thousand years ago.

Somehow the message of both gifts seemed very much alike to me that Christmas Eve—the ageless and urgent message of communicating love.

14
Last Names Are Not Important

The weather report said there was a good possibility of sleet—severe weather for Georgia, even in December. I had gotten our four children off to school looking at the ominous sky and shivering in the doorway as the bus pulled away. I poured myself another cup of coffee and watched the birds eating crumbs I had thrown in the backyard. What a nice day to stay at home.

The telephone interrupted my thoughts.

"Marion, Dyanne's mother is in a real bad way. She's in so much pain and has been in the hospital for such a long time, now—and Dyanne is about all to pieces. I thought you might—pray."

The call was from my hairdresser, Carolyn. She knew by the books I took to the beauty shop and bits of conversation that I was really turned on to what God could do in a life and situation.

Dyanne was a woman I had gotten to know only slightly because we went to the beauty shop on the same day. We didn't seem to have a lot in common. She loved Little League ball, which made me uncomfortable. And she liked to cook and could sew.

I knew from the beauty shop conversation that her mother had been a diabetic for years and was almost blind. Now, a sore on her leg wouldn't heal, and the doctors saw no way around amputation. Her mother was young, only in her fifties. Caught in the middle of agonizing pain and relentless fear, each day had become a nightmare. She had been in the hospital for over two months.

One day in the beauty shop I asked Dyanne if I could put her mother on my prayer list and share it with others in my prayer group. "Oh, yes," she whispered in a soft voice. Then she came over to my chair and slowly spelled the name for me. "C-a-t-h-e-r-i-n-e L-e-o-n-a-r-d." She added, "Thank you so much," after I wrote the name.

Now Carolyn repeated the question over the phone, "Will you pray and maybe call someone else to pray too?"

"Of course," I answered quickly. But already God had spoken to my heart. *Are you willing to do more than pray here in your kitchen?*

"It looks like sleet, Lord. I don't know Dyanne very well. Why, I don't even know her last name. Surely there must be others."

I didn't ask about her last name.

"Carolyn, maybe Venera and I can go to the hospital."

"Oh, that would be wonderful. Will you call Venera?"

"Yes, I'll call. Thanks for telling me about Dyanne."

"Lord, Venera's so funny about traveling in bad weather and she doesn't even think I'm a good driver. This is her husband's day off. She won't want to go with me," I prayed.

Sighing, I dialed her familiar number. She listened as I related Carolyn's message. She knew Dyanne slightly from the beauty shop, also. "They're supposed to operate this morning. Do you think you might go with me to the hospital?"

"I'll pray and call you back."

Venera called back and said without enthusiasm that she wanted to go with me. "Looks like snow," she added.

I glanced around at my dirty kitchen, got dressed and drove over to pick up Venera. We rode in silence. My

windshield wipers didn't work well and I leaned forward
to see. She told me curtly that I was driving too fast.
For a moment I thought about increasing my speed, but
lifted my foot off the gas. She always tells me how to
drive, I thought. Then God seemed to remind me, Satan
would love for you two not to be united on this mission.
No time to be petty.

I spoke, after slowing down, "Do you think we're
supposed to be going?"

She laughed, "If we're going on feelings, no. We don't
even know Dyanne's last name. Looks like the rain is
freezing now on the windshield. But since when could
Christians go on feelings?"

I nodded, slowing down even more. We drove into
the parking lot. Holding our heads down against the cold
rain and wind, we walked in silence to the hospital
clutching some fruit and candy we had brought for
Dyanne.

We got off the elevator on the third floor and spotted
Dyanne and her family standing in the hall. She looked
as though she were in terrible pain. I realized then that
I had almost never seen Dyanne when she wasn't laughing.
She greeted us warmly and responded to our impromtu
hugs. Dyanne introduced us to her father, Earl Leonard,
and other relatives. They all greeted us with enthusiasm
and gratitude. Then she explained the situation. The
doctors were about to operate but her mother had suffered
severe chest pains. Now they were afraid there might
be a blood clot in her lung and surgery would have to
be postponed. And still, Dyanne's mother wouldn't agree
to the amputation of her leg.

Dyanne looked terribly tired. There was nowhere to
sit. "Have you eaten?" I asked. She shook her head,
indicating that she hadn't. "Come on down the hall to
the lounge and let us get you some food." She hesitated

and looked at other family members as people do who are too tired to make even a minor decision. They urged her to go with us.

We sat in the lounge on bright orange modern furniture. We brought Dyanne a sandwich and a cup of coffee. She ate it slowly, without seeming to taste it, talking and crying softly as she ate.

Then I got the definite message from God that we were to unite in prayer. Venera will suggest it, I assured myself and God. She's bolder than I am. I'm not sure how to go about praying here with all these people around. I looked at Venera but she didn't seem about to suggest anything. My heart pounded—a sure sign that God wanted me to suggest prayer. I heard myself ask, "May we pray with you?" Dyanne nodded her head quickly, reached out for both our hands, and shut her eyes.

I held her hand leaning forward in my chair. Venera dropped to her knees and grabbed Dyanne's hand and mine. Nurses and visitors walked past in the hall.

I asked God to give Dyanne strength and knowledge that he loved her and her mother and cared deeply that she suffered. Then I prayed for the doctors and specifically that the surgery wouldn't have to be postponed—and that Jesus would be glorified. I asked for fear to be removed from Dyanne's mother and that she be willing to lose her leg if that were part of God's healing process.

Venera agreed with me and asked that Jesus become real to Dyanne's mother in a new way. She asked for peace for Dyanne's father. I was all ready for Venera to close the prayer when Dyanne cried out, "Dear Lord, thank you for these two dear friends who have come. I needed someone so much. None of my friends are here. Thank you for giving me my mother for this long. We want your will above all else."

Her prayer of gratitude continued. It wasn't fearful or begging, but of praise. We opened our eyes and wiped away tears.

We walked back down the hall to learn that X-rays had confirmed that Dyanne's mother didn't have a blood clot. It must have been nerves the doctors decided. She seemed much better. They operated, but didn't amputate, merely scraped the dead tissue away. However, a month later surgery was performed again, and this time the doctors did amputate her leg. Catherine agreed to the amputation.

She was dismissed from the hospital on a prematurely beautiful spring-like day in January. A few jonquils bloomed. She smiled gratefully to be outside again, even if she was in a wheelchair.

Venera and I had so many good reasons to turn back. But we couldn't seem to remember them when Dyanne thanked God there in that waiting room for the two dear friends who had come to be with her.

15
The Wrong Number

"No, I'm not the Mrs. Hammond you want," the sharp disgruntled voice snapped. "Some of you people from the church are always dialing my number by mistake. Why can't you look up numbers correctly? We used to go to church there, but you don't care about old people like us. And I'm tired of your calling here." Calling from our church directory, I had phoned the wrong Mrs. Hammond.

She can't talk to me like that. I don't have to take it, I thought. But as I prepared to hang up, God spoke to my heart. *Don't hang up. Reach out to her. You haven't dialed the wrong number. Talk to her. I'll help you. Don't turn away.*

Quickly I thought, well what approach will I use? Maybe humor, I decided even though I didn't see how anything could reach her.

"I care about old people. They're fun. One of my friends at church is in her mid-seventies. I'll bet you aren't that old," I said in a slightly teasing voice.

"No, but I'm old. You don't have time for old people," she snapped.

"You certainly don't sound old. I think you're fooling me."

"No, I'm not. If you could see me, you would know I'm old."

"I'd love to see you. May I come over one morning?" I was shocked at my suggestion. I'm shy. It didn't sound like me at all.

There was a silence, a long silence. Then it was as though another woman spoke over the phone. The voice was soft, warm. "Yes, oh, yes. When can you come?"

By then I had become so enthralled with our strange conversation that I wanted to blurt out, "Right now"; throw down the phone and rush over to her house. But I managed, "How about Tuesday morning?"

"Fine, fine. I'll bet you forget."

"No I won't. It'll be early though, just after I drop my twins off at kindergarten."

"I'll be looking for you," her gentle voice insisted.

By Tuesday I wasn't feeling friendly or helpful at all. I felt foolish for having suggested the visit. Why hadn't I just hung up? She'll think I'm some kind of a nut. I think I am, too. But I'm a dependable nut, I reasoned. I'll do whatever I promise.

A few minutes after nine I drove up into the Hammond's driveway. My eyes traveled over the lush green yard filled with azaleas and dogwood. A patio adjoined the carport and overlooked a dew-filled grassy backyard. Birds and squirrels were everywhere in the tall pines and hardwoods. For a moment I squinted my eyes in the bright sun that reflected from spotless white patio furniture. I noticed an abundance of green plants that thrived in attractive small containers. The friendly surroundings helped my fear some, but still I rang the doorbell with apprehension.

Right away the door opened and a small woman with keen eyes looked up at me. "Well, how old do you think I am?" She was smiling and I liked her right away, but I didn't think she was the type to play games with.

"Between sixty and sixty-five," I answered back quite honestly.

"Seventy," she snapped in a friendly, teasing way.

I laughed, in open amazement, as my fear ebbed away. "Come in," she insisted.

We sat at the kitchen table and drank coffee. I wasn't sure what to talk about, but felt it definitely wasn't the time to say, "You should come back to church." Somehow we discovered we both loved animals fiercely. We went to the glass door in the den and looked out at the bird feeder in her yard. She pointed out her pet squirrel who was practically tame.

Ruth and Ed lived alone in the lovely home. They had no children, although I could tell from the way she asked about mine, and listened intently with twinkling eyes, that she loved them.

We forgot that we hadn't known each other for years and talked freely. "Some days I go to the mailbox when I see one of my neighbors out, hoping she'll wave to me. We came from a friendly neighborhood. We've only been here a short while. I miss my friends. I need people," Ruth said, in open honesty that I admired. Then abruptly she got up and offered me more coffee and changed the subject back to dogs and cats.

Nearly two hours passed before I stood to leave. She walked to the door with her arm around me. "Will you come back?"

"Of course, and you must come to see me. I'll bring my husband over sometime to meet yours. I want to meet him, too. I'll even bring all my children, if you think you can stand them."

"Oh, yes," she cried, and clapped her hands together.

That was two years ago. Since then Ruth and Ed have met my family. I've been back to visit often. During one visit she gave me a beautiful fern and she passes along her *Humane Society* magazines to me. Once she handed me a basket I admired. We chat on the phone often.

Recently, we sat at her kitchen table. Without warning

we were laughing one moment and shedding tears the next. "The Lord sent you here. I know he did. Bless you for coming," Ruth said, with some difficulty.

Just recently I got a note from her. I've memorized the last two lines . . . "feel sure it's due to a great extent to the prayers and loving thoughts of our friends. Don't give up on me—'cause I do love and appreciate you."

I've thanked God many times for allowing me to dial that wrong number and hear what Ruth was really saying, "I'm lonely."

16
Gyp's Tribute

I wasn't quite two when my daddy died. Just before the funeral they took me to see my father's body and the many beautiful flowers. I don't remember it, of course, but sometimes it seems that I can remember being overwhelmed by the flowers that surrounded and towered above me.

Through the years my mother has often told me about the lovely flowers. And she has related that when I was lifted up to see my father, I whispered, "He's asleep."

By the time I came to realize that my daddy hadn't been asleep, an intense dislike for massive floral offerings had crept into my heart. I was probably seven or so when I found out that there was no "back side" to funeral flowers—only hard, green Styrofoam, wire, and a few leaves. The discovery infuriated me and my dislike for funeral flowers became even stronger.

Now, over thirty-five years since my father's death, I still tend to shrink away from these kind of flowers—as though they are something vile. Looking at them, I feel something between anger and grief. And for as long as I can remember each time I see these kinds of flowers the words, "it's not enough," have popped into my mind.

What's not enough, I've asked myself over and over? Surely there were enough flowers at my father's funeral. They had trouble getting them all inside the church. Enough mourners? The pews had been filled with friends.

A nameless ache that goes beyond the loss of my father

has remained stubbornly in my heart and I can't pinpoint what has bothered me all these years about the flowers at my father's funeral. I've argued with myself time and time again about the childlike hatred I've harbored for the perfectly proportioned floral offerings that are sent to funerals. And I've really tried to learn to appreciate them. Yet, they remain in my eyes, staunch, uniform—almost like soldiers lined up for inspection.

Sitting at a funeral recently, I reasoned that the symmetrically arranged flowers conveyed friends' sympathy. Yes, of course, they're sorry, the unreasonable part of me retorted—but what else? Just being sorry isn't enough—and neither are the mammoth arrangements of flowers with their "back sides" missing.

I once watched three employees from the funeral home load the floral offerings into their van to haul them to the cemetery. The men handled the flowers like boys at the supermarket sacking groceries on a busy Saturday. I wanted to look away, but I watched painfully and remained silent as they slammed the door and sped down the highway. A few flowers remained scattered on the paved driveway. Looking down at the broken stems the words, "it's not enough," once again plowed through my mind, haunting me.

My mother and I were talking not long ago. It was in the spring of the year and she remembered the month my father had died—May. Once again she spoke about the beautiful flowers at his funeral. That uneasy feeling began to stir in me. But then, glancing at my mother, I got the distinct impression that this time she was going to remember something she had never told me before. She wasn't really looking at me as she remembered and I listened almost without breathing.

"I guess of all the flowers there, I never got to see the ones that meant the most to me. Gyp White had been a carnival man and one year he stayed on in our little town because he said he was tired of traveling. Gyp was unusual. People often ignored him, said he was a nuisance. A shy man who tried desperately to please, he never seemed to fit in anywhere. His appearance was shabby, almost comical—you know?

I nodded, beginning to see him in my mind—the hard lines around his thin mouth standing out on his weather-beaten face. His eyes held unspoken sadness, yet remained ready to come alive with instant joy if encouraged.

My mother continued, still not really looking at me. "Someone told me after the funeral that when Gyp heard about your father's death, he went out and bought a new white linen handkerchief. He wore it underneath his coat across his chest because he didn't own a white shirt. Gyp came to the funeral in a taxi. Your daddy was Gyp's friend. He had picked wild flowers and brought them to the service."

My heart thumped wildly and my throat suddenly ached. Now I could see the colorful, slightly limp flowers clutched in Gyp's gnarled, tanned hand.

"Well, when Gyp got to the funeral and saw the people were dressed so finely and that such exquisite flowers had been sent from the florist, he left, taking his small bouquet with him."

I nodded silently and determined not to cry then. And when I finally did, my tears were of longed-for release and profound gratitude. It may have seemed that Gyp had turned back, but his quiet act of love had finally come to my attention and I've smiled to myself with deep satisfaction since my mother told me that story.

Gyp White, a carnival man I had never known had picked a handful of flowers for his beloved friend, my daddy—and at last, *it was enough*.

17
The No-Turning-Back Kit

Ten minutes before our regular Sunday night Church Training class at church was to be dismissed, Brenda dropped a bombshell.

I had admired her honesty since we first met. Soft-spoken, gentle, a bit shy, but very observant, Brenda had a way of not sugarcoating anything she wanted to ask or say. She got right to the point and asked questions with an almost childlike innocence and enthusiasm.

Brenda was a new Christian and as excited about her personal relationship with Jesus as a child on the last day of school. She loved to discover new truths about spiritual matters. She had grown with amazing speed in her understanding of the Christian walk.

Brenda had been on a mountaintop for several weeks and I had tried to tell her about the valleys—make her understand that she was bound to tumble into one. I wanted her to know that she musn't depend on her feelings when she took a tumble.

I had often spoken of coming down off the mountaintop and she would nod, grinning, and I got the impression that Brenda didn't think it would happen to her. "So much has changed around our house," she told me. "I've given up my job to stay home with the children. I'm so happy with them. Roy's stopped smoking, too, and is reading the Bible. We sit around and talk about God. I'm sharing with my neighbors what Jesus is doing in my life . . . and I just can't read enough of God's Word.

How did I miss this for so long?"

"About the valley, Brenda . . ."

But she didn't seem to hear. She went on telling me of more miracles that God was performing in her home. I rejoiced with Brenda.

I had noticed that Brenda came into the Church Training class looking a little tense, her face more set than usual. Her smiling eyes didn't dart around the room acknowledging new friends. But I had reasoned, Sundays can be tiring as well as exciting. Then just before the class was over she asked the shocking question, slowly, softly. "Can someone help me? I've come tonight to see if someone can show me why I shouldn't chuck it all—go back to my old way of life.

"We're out of groceries. I haven't eaten all day. I'm hungry. My husband cut down a tree and it fell on our neighbor's fence. She's bringing over our supper tonight because Roy's grandfather died. Except for her we wouldn't have supper. Roy and I have argued all day long—all week in fact. I'm so tired of fussing. My baby's been sick all week. So have I. I hate my kitchen floor. It's coming apart and I can't stand it any more. I've had it with the Christian life. I've never suffered so much. Why shouldn't I . . . just turn back?"

The class was a small group of women. None of us turned to look at Brenda. While my heart ached for her, I praised God for her beautiful honesty.

The teacher, Dawn Johnson, wasn't shaken by Brenda's plea for help. Dawn continued smiling and nodded her head in understanding. She explained to Brenda how Satan wanted her to turn back, and how all new Christians come under this attack. Dawn didn't lead Brenda to believe that her circumstances would automatically change, but rather gave her Scripture from the sixth chapter of Romans and stressed the fact that we can have victory through Jesus in any circumstance.

Out in the hall after we had been dismissed, I didn't know exactly what to say to Brenda, so I reached over and hugged her and said, "I love you."

"Oh, Marion, I'm afraid I'm not going to make it. I can't live the Christian life. Haven't I suffered enough?"

"Remember his suffering."

"On the cross?" she asked with tears streaming down her face. She thought for a moment.

I could barely hear her answer, "No, I haven't suffered enough."

The next morning I awoke with Brenda on my mind. Surely there was something physical I could do for her. She had refused my offer last night to run by the grocery store and pick up a few things. Not knowing exactly what I was going to say, I phoned her. She sounded good, steady, calm, even bright and cheery.

"Guess what?" she asked. "Dawn called early this morning and invited us to have supper with them tonight. I don't think we can go because of Roy's work, but wasn't that sweet of her?"

Suddenly I heard myself ask, "Can I come over for lunch? I'll stop by the grocery store and pick up whatever looks good."

"Sure," she responded, "sounds like fun."

Food's not enough, came the powerful thought. Right, I agreed, but what else? I thought for a moment. I would take my favorite record—the one by Gloria and Bill Gaither, "Alluleia." And Brenda loves to read. What one book do I have that is in a category by itself and is appropriate for right now? Simple choice, "The Christian's Secret of a Happy Life," by Hannah Whitall Smith. Checking my rosebush I discovered three lovely rosebuds still fresh with dew.

At the grocery store I bought soft drinks, ham, cheese,

rye bread, a big dill pickle, and a bag of freshly-baked cookies.

Finally, I stood at Brenda's back door holding all the things I had brought, and ringing the doorbell with my elbow.

She opened the door, looked at me and laughed, "What in the world have you got?"

Right then, I suddenly knew for the first time what I had brought. God had helped me assemble it. I answered, "It's a no-turning-back kit!"

"Well, bring it on in," Brenda smiled, knowing what I meant.

About a week later, when we could talk about it, Brenda told me, "I played the record over and over and read the book as soon as you left. I learned something. There's a purpose to suffering. It's just a necessary part of the Christian life. And I knew before I finished the book that I couldn't turn back—no matter what. She smiled and said softly, "There's really no turning back, is there?"

PART FOUR—SUFFERING

Though he slay me, yet will I trust him (Job 13:15, KJV).

18
Soldiers Come in all Sizes

I can't honestly say which I noticed first—the child's beautifully radiant face or the fact that he practically ran on crutches.

Ricky and his mother, Bobbie Griffin, were out-of-town visitors at our church. Nancy Abbott had brought them and I knew immediately who they were. Nancy often spoke about Ricky. He had been born with an open spine. He had his first operation when he was only two days old. The doctors told his mother that he probably wouldn't live through surgery. Bobbie had waited throughout the night and when she received word that her son had made it, new hope for his life became alive in her heart, despite the doctor's grave warnings. There would have to be many more operations and still, Ricky would probably never walk.

Bobbie wasn't married and even though she realized that a child needs both a mother and a father, she knew before her child was born that she couldn't go through life wondering if he were being taken care of—loved. When Bobbie learned of her baby's serious birth defect, she became even more determined to see that he had the things in life he needed—and a chance for happiness.

I watched Ricky hurrying about the church on his small crutches. Then I saw his mother watching him. She looked at Ricky as though she couldn't quite believe what she saw. A quiet pride and joy seemed ready to explode from her face.

Nancy, a staff member of Crippled Children's Clinic in Atlanta, brought Bobbie and Ricky over to meet me. Tears sparkled in Nancy's eyes as she made the introductions. Ricky was very special to her. She had watched his amazing progress since birth.

"Hi," Ricky looked up at me and grinned as though I were somebody really special.

"Hi, Ricky. I'm so happy to finally meet you," I said.

His silent grin seemed to say, "Yeah, great. Got to hurry on. Bye." And he was off again. Breathtakingly beautiful with golden hair that slanted across his smooth forehead, he seemed to almost glow. Yet, he was unmistakably all boy. Bobbie's eyes left Ricky for a moment and she gave me her full attention. She spoke softly, yet amazingly warm and her simple, "Hello," made me smile more than I had expected to. Her voice matched her looks—small, gentle, a bit shy. "Better see if I can catch up with my son," she joked. And when she looked at him once again that special look of uncontained joy spread over her face as though they were being reunited after a lengthy separation.

"Just look at him," Nancy marveled. "Puts on those braces every morning as routinely as other seven-year-olds put on their shoes. He's a walking miracle. Most determined little fellow I've ever met."

I nodded, watching him rush about the church, leaning on the crutches for a moment as he spoke to someone, then he was off again.

Two months later on Christmas Eve, Nancy told some of us at church, "Ricky's sick. He's on the way to Egleston Hospital now in an ambulance. Pray. He's a mighty sick little boy."

Ricky and his mother lived nearby in Athens, Georgia, about sixty-five miles from the Atlanta Children's Hospital. As word of his grave illness spread throughout our church and community, many began praying.

Ricky arrived at the hospital unconscious. His heart had nearly stopped as the ambulance sped them there. Egleston is full of desperately sick children—even at Christmas. Bobbie quietly joined the other parents and began the long, painful wait, prayerfully.

Ricky came to after several hours for a short time and he and his mother were alone in his room. All the doctors and nurses had left for a few moments. Ricky spoke to his mother telling her that he was very tired. He asked her to lay her head down on the pillow beside him. Then he said he wanted to pray, but was too tired. He asked her to say the words for him.

Bobbie prayed, "Now I lay me down to sleep . . ."

Ricky slept for a few moments, then opened his eyes and asked, "Mother, will you come with me?"

"Where are you going?" she asked.

"On a trip. Will you come?"

Bobbie answered softly, "I'll always be with you." And he slept again.

We got reports on Ricky from Nancy. He would slip a little, then regain the ground he had lost. He lapsed into unconsciousness, but still fought. Ricky was used to doing the impossible and didn't understand defeat.

However, his lack of progress registered clearly on Nancy's face. She was allowed into Intensive Care with him daily. Bobbie refused to leave her son. She said they would leave the hospital together. For nearly two weeks, she kept a vigil over him. Once again he spoke, "If you loved me, you would give me some water." But then he became the encourager squeezing his mother's hand tightly and smiling through half closed eyes. Bobbie understood his message, "I'm 'gonna make it. Don't worry."

As Bobbie waited and prayed, it rained each day. The sun refused to shine. Everything looked gray and murky outside the hospital. Inside, Christmas decorations were evident and Bobbie's eyes carefully avoided them.

A week before Ricky had become ill, he had said, "Mother, 'ya know when I get to heaven, I'll just throw away these crutches and run like everyone else. I won't be a cripple anymore. Won't that be great!"

Bobbie had agreed, a little surprised, but not too shocked at Ricky's profound statement. He had accepted Jesus as his Savior when he was five and to him Jesus and heaven were as real as his friends and the school he attended.

Teachers at the Athens Christian school that he attended marveled at his deep understanding of spiritual matters. Ricky had recently shared enthusiastically with two adults how to just "invite Jesus into your heart—he'll come," and now they were active Christians.

When Bobbie took Ricky to the school as a prospective student, the headmaster, Buhl Cumming, had wondered how such a little fellow could manage all the stairs with crutches. He seemed so determined that they decided to let him try—for a while, anyway. Ricky had climbed the steps with amazing speed and without complaint. At a spring program during his first year at the school Ricky was assigned the part of the master of ceremonies in a play. With great determination and courage he walked out onto the stage smiling—without his crutches.

I went to see Bobbie in the hospital. She sat in the waiting room alone. She had changed so much through her son's illness that I scarcely recognized her. But when she stood and smiled at me, I knew it was Bobbie. We met and embraced silently. Then we sat by the window and looked out at the rain. She talked about what a special Christmas it would be when she got her son home. The only complaint I heard her make was about the continuous rain. "Oh, I wish the sun would shine," she said softly.

Daily we heard about Ricky through Nancy. He slipped deeper and deeper into a coma. His vital signs dropped still lower and in a desperate attempt to save his life, the doctors operated.

In the operating room on January 6, 1975, Ricky's tired heart stopped. The busy little body that had rushed through life almost as though he knew he didn't have much time, was finally still. Bobbie left the hospital, but not before she thanked each doctor and nurse who had worked with Ricky. She thanked aides, maids, everyone. Several of the doctors had been unable to hold back their tears. Bobbie said good-bye to the mothers still waiting with their sick children. She assured them she would continue to pray for their recovery.

The funeral was held in the foothills of the mountains of North Georgia. It was a cold, rainy day—sleet threatened. Bobbie had requested no flowers, except those wishing to do so, might send a single red rosebud.

At the funeral home containers of red rosebuds nearly filled the room. And in Ricky's lapel—a red rosebud. It had been sent to him by his little buddy, David, from Crippled Children's Clinic. David always told Ricky, "Someday I want to walk on my crutches just as good as you do." And watching Ricky, he kept trying.

I had only seen Ricky one time in our church, rushing about on his crutches. Now the bright blond hair was carefully combed and the incredible stillness of death seemed almost too much to fathom.

As we sat in the funeral home waiting for time to go to the church, a teenager sobbed softly and someone told me that it was Ricky's baby-sitter and cousin. They had been great pals. Her sobs grew louder. Bobbie got up and walked over to the girl and knelt down by her side. I could hear even though she barely whispered. "Hey, you know what Ricky used to say about crying women,

'Can't stand 'em.' Smile, honey. Smile for Ricky. He would like that.''

The youngster's sobs hushed slowly and she smiled hesitantly—then finally really smiled at Bobbie.

" 'Atta girl," Bobbie encouraged, patting her shoulder. Then walking back to where she had been sitting between her parents, I saw the smile evaporate from her face and the agony return. Periodically Bobbie walked to the small casket and adjusted Ricky's coat, patted his shoulder, or simply touched his hair.

I slipped a Christmas card out of my purse and looked at it once again. It was of a pastel watercoloring showing a green grassy hill where the sun shone warmly. A strong, yet gentle figure, unmistakably Jesus, stood on the top of the hill, smiling. He leaned over and reached forth his hand to help an eager little boy with bright hair scramble to the top of the hill. The child's outstretched hand almost touched the hand of Jesus. I gave it to a relative and asked her to give it to Bobbie after the funeral.

Then it was time to go to the church.

In the sanctuary the organist played, "Safe in the Arms of Jesus," and I was glad I had decided to bring the card to Bobbie.

The headmaster from Ricky's school, The Reverend Cumming, spoke at the service after two other ministers had shared. He remembered Ricky in a warm, informal way—almost as though he spoke to only one person—and almost as if nothing at all had happened to Ricky. Smiling and remembering he said, "The last time I saw Ricky was when he left for the Christmas holidays. He waved good-bye to me and grinned. Then he called out, 'See 'ya next year.' He turned and rushed down the hall, mingling with the other students and singing at the top of his voice, 'Onward Christian Soldiers.' ''

The funeral ended and the church filled with the triumphant song Bobbie had requested—"Onward Christian Soldiers."

As I listened the song spoke to me differently than it ever had before. I made up my own words to it, even though they didn't fit the music.

"Onward Christian soldiers that I've left behind. Onward now, it's important that you continue to move forward, even though I can't march with you any more right now. You just march on till we're together again. Keep moving forward everyone—Mother—don't turn back because of the pain. Don't ever turn back . . ."

19
The Bridge Builder

"America! I'm really here," Ursina had murmured, "if only my family could visit this wonderful land. My dream all my life is to come here." Her eyes glistened slightly with tears, "I'm really here!" She opened her arms as if to hug someone. When she talked about America with such intensity, I would look around at my small hometown of Elberton, Georgia, wondering if Ursina saw something I had missed.

She often spoke about her mother, brother, and sister, and her country fondly, but if she suffered from homesickness, she never let any of us know. Ursina's father had died in a Russian prison in 1945.

She knew a lot about American history, but never flaunted her knowledge. Always though, she wanted to learn more about our land and customs. She listened enraptured as we answered her never ending questions. "I want to learn all about America." Ursina pronounced America in a special, almost reverent way. Nothing ever seemed too small to captivate her attention.

Ursina's accent fascinated me. I hadn't met many people from other countries, and no one my own age. I watched her mouth closely as she pronounced my name precisely.

Sometimes now I don't think about her for months—even years. Then something stirs my memory—an old song, a ballerina skirt pulled out of mothballs, or a photograph of our graduating class. Then I recall vividly my senior year of high school, in 1953, and Ursina Stahnke, the German exchange student, who had come to live in America for a year and to graduate with our class.

The stubborn memory has remained in my heart all these years and with fondness, I painfully remember Ursina. She could have easily been a beauty queen with her long, thick hair and dark eyes. Her flawless complexion seemed to be as perfect as doll's skin. When she smiled, it happened slowly, like a velvet curtain being drawn back. She seemed completely unaware of her deep beauty.

The Halls, the family she was living with in Elberton, fell in love with Ursina almost instantly. Mrs. Hall sewed beautifully and as a school party approached, began making Ursina an exquisite formal gown. Ursina told me about it. "So lovely, new, green net, wonderfully soft . . ." she had whispered, with tears sparkling in her eyes. "I'm going to have my picture made in it for my family."

One bright September day when Ursina had been here only four weeks, some of us girls in the senior class decided to have a party for her. We called it a coke party. We planned to have the get-together at Shirley's home. We all brought something special we had baked and there was an air of excitement.

Ursina came into the room a bit breathless, a little nervous, looked around at us, then slowly smiled that wonderful smile of hers, obviously pleased at our efforts. She tasted the cakes and cookies with great fanfare, as though she were judging a cooking contest, and she raved over each morsel. I watched her lift a coke bottle to her mouth. She swallowed slowly, then smiled approvingly. Ursina got the most out of everything. I had gulped mine down without even tasting it. When all of her coke was gone, she shut one eye and looked into the empty bottle with the other eye as though she peered into a microscope and saw something fascinating.

Ursina planned to ride Shirley's pet horse that afternoon. She was a skilled rider. As I left the party, she called out, "Bye; see 'ya tomorrow." Ursina had started to pick up our Southern slang and it pleased her and us.

That night I received a telephone call. One of my girl friends spoke in a strange, tight voice. "Marion, Ursina fell or was thrown off the horse this afternoon. She's in the hospital, unconscious. They're going to operate, I think. They—they—shaved her head."

Back in bed I rationalized and hoped, since they've shaved her head, they surely will operate and she will be fine. I went to sleep imagining a smiling Ursina with short, curly hair.

The next morning I learned the agonizing truth. The news spread grimly throughout our shocked town.

Ursina had died.

I shut my eyes remembering her peeping down into the empty coke bottle and grinning. I remembered how her eyes sparkled when tears threatened. I thought about how coming to America had been her life's dream. My small hometown had been America for Ursina.

I couldn't cry. I ached inside, unable to shed tears.

Then I began to think about her mother—what bitterness she must have for people in Elberton—America.

Elberton mourned. At the funeral home Ursina's body was never left alone. They had dressed her in the new green evening gown she had never gotten to wear. Later at a memorial service, a granite statue of Ursina, chiseled by a gifted artist from Elberton, was placed in the school yard and a well-known columnist from Atlanta spoke. She wrote about Ursina and Elberton in her column. Our senior class dedicated the annual to Ursina's memory. We used the picture of her in the new green dress. She would never see those photographs. Underneath the picture it said, "Ursina Stahnke, beloved German exchange student who was accidentally killed while horseback riding on September 17, 1953—to know her was to love her."

Many people from Elberton sent messages of sympathy to Ursina's family in Hamburg, Germany. I couldn't write a letter. It seemed incredible to me that her mother wanted to hear from Americans. How she must hate us!

I tried to pray for them. Maybe prayer is an attitude of the heart after all and God understands a silent, aching heart that doesn't know the exact words to say to him.

A prayer that I hadn't known how to express was answered through a letter from Ursina's mother. Our local newspaper published it.[1] Reading the letter, feelings I couldn't put into words welled up inside me and I finally cried for a long time.

The weeks in America have been the crown of Ursina's life. She loved America before she had seen it. America had always been the goal of her thoughts and desires. I had only jubilant letters from her. She seemed to live in a dream, she was drunk with joy about the lovable people in Elberton. Ursina drank in all the beauty and was enjoying life in a manner that she never had been able to in our narrow circumstances. It could not have become any more beautiful perhaps—therefore, my beloved child had to go. She came home very much differently from what we had pictured. On the 25th of September we saw the child once more—like Snow White lying in her coffin, but already quite distant and sublime. We became quiet and prayerful at her sight.

[1] Excerpt of letter published in *The Elberton Star*, Elberton, Georgia, November 10, 1953.

The chapel had been turned into a sea of sunflowers at my wish and it was filled with music, "Andante" by Hayden. I chose the twenty-third Psalm for the minister to read, and later learned that you also had chosen that Scripture for her in Elberton.

I don't feel anything but gratitude for the people of Elberton for helping Ursina realize her dream. How beautifully and how lovely you sent me my child! Your acts of love are a wall around my heart. I have become quiet. God would have taken her here too—I know this for certain.

Please give Ursina's clothes to poor children in Elberton.

I will by and by write more letters to Elberton. We don't ever want to miss the love of friends that spoke to us from letters. My children and I greet all the dear people of Elberton. We are more often with you now than here, as if we could still reach Ursina there. There shall remain a bridge of affection which my beloved child has built between our people.

Ursina's family later crossed that bridge and came to Elberton for a visit. I was out of town and didn't meet them. But I already knew them. They were people, like Ursina, with amazing love for my country. They were people who simply would not turn their backs on my town, my country.

As time passed, I often caught myself looking for beauty in the simplest places, expecting happiness out of heartache, and experiencing forgiveness where bitterness might have grown.

20
Season of Courage

On Christmas Day, 1972, eleven-year-old Ricky Shadburn ran down the road to his friend's house. The driver of a car approaching from the rear saw Ricky running and attempted to slow down. As his foot touched the brake, the car skidded into Ricky. Someone ran for Ricky's mother.

Many people in the little town of Cumming, Georgia, joined in praying for Ricky as they heard of the tragedy.

At the hospital, doctors gave the Shadburns no hope whatsoever. The prayers continued through the night. Ricky clung to life to the amazement of the doctors.

In intensive care they hooked Ricky onto a breathing machine. A tracheotomy was performed, catheter, and food tubes inserted.

For twenty-six days Ricky's parents followed the doctor's instructions. "Just walk in, look at him and walk out. Don't touch him or say a word—not even his name."

During these visits Ricky didn't move or open his eyes. Finally the respirator was removed and Ricky breathed on his own! Much of his body remained paralyzed and his arms and legs twisted.

Doctors told the Shadburns he would receive proper care in a nursing home.

His heartsick mother asked with concern, "Can they do more for Ricky than we can?"

"No, he'll receive much better care from you—if you can do it."

"We can do it," Betty Shadburn said with determination.

The doctors warned the parents not to expect anything in the way of improvement.

Fifty-six days after the accident Ricky went home. His mother spoke to him in a natural, loving way, as if he understood every word. She asked him questions every day—for almost a year. There wasn't a flicker of response.

A gurgling noise meant Ricky was choking to death. The Shadburns had a few seconds to suction his throat. Once he turned blue as they worked with him. After that Betty's legs and feet remained swollen much of the time from her constant vigil.

Ricky's little brother quickly assumed the role of big brother, talking to Ricky, touching him, and sharing secrets with him. Still, there was no response. Ricky's older brother began helping with the many household duties, freeing his mother to care for Ricky. He lifted Ricky, carrying him to the car for visits to the doctor.

Lelan Shadburn assumed the painful job of giving his son therapy—painful for both Ricky and his father. Ricky screamed in pain as his bent, drawn limbs were straightened over and over.

On a beautiful day in November 1973, the Shadburns took Ricky outdoors to see his pet pony. As Ricky looked at his pet, tears streamed down his face. It had been nearly a year, but Ricky had responded.

After that he began to respond to the questions his mother asked. He shook his head "No," smiled, and nodded "yes."

On a cold, rainy day in December 1973, three members of my Sunday School class went to visit Ricky. We took homemade cakes, candy, fruit, and more of the life-sustaining milk formula he had to have. Our class sent a card and enclosed a small amount of money. My husband's Sunday School class of thirteen-year-old boys sent a card and a small contribution.

On the spur of the moment I had painted a large greeting card on poster paper for Ricky, depicting animals in a jungle.

Betty Shadburn held the door open for us. I formed my first impression. Oh, she looks so bright, so strong—just like any mother—maybe even more cheerful than most on this gloomy day.

She was neat and her face seemed radiant. Her soft, brown hair was short. I looked at her hands, thinking how much they must do for Ricky and her family.

She urged, "Come see Ricky."

We followed her into the living room where Ricky's hospital bed had been moved. "Look, Ricky, you have company."

He turned slowly toward us and smiled. All at once Ricky wasn't a little boy far off somewhere. He was right in front of me, smiling. I propped the large card up on his chest. "I made this for you." He smiled. "Do you like it?" He nodded, looking from one animal to another.

His mother required more of him. "Ricky, where's the lion?"

Slowly he pointed with his bent wrist and touched the lion.

"Good," we all cheered.

"The zebra?" Betty asked. His eyes found it first; then his arms touched it. He identified each animal.

"Oh, if he could just speak one word," his mother said with deep longing. "I believe he will. I haven't asked God for anything he hasn't given me. For months I prayed he could nod his head. Look at him now!"

I looked at Ricky imagining his first word . . . "Mama."

"Time to eat, Ricky," Betty announced.

Gently, Betty Shadburn lifted the covers off of Ricky's

stomach. She knew the procedure of feeding him so well. She talked with us, only glancing at the tube going into Ricky's stomach twice. I watched in awe as she poured the liquid directly into the tube that fed Ricky. I tried .to imagine myself in her place. I couldn't.

Suddenly, he cried in pain. "His arm's twisted under him," Betty explained. But she stood still, saying, "Ricky, put your hand on your stomach." Slowly he moved the arm himself until it rested on his stomach, flashing a big smile at his mother.

Betty thought of another accomplishment, "Ricky— Monday, Tuesday, Wednesday, Friday, Sat . . ." but he interrupted her, shaking his head furiously. Then she recited it again correctly, and he nodded, rewarding us with a joyful smile.

Soon we had to leave. "Tell them good-bye, Ricky," Betty urged. He leaned toward us one at a time lifting his bent arms to us. As we leaned down toward him, Ricky squeezed with all his strength.

As we left, he winked at us.

In the kitchen as we put on our coats, Betty's shoulders slumped a bit. Tears glistened in her eyes. "It's been over a year now and neighbors, friends, even strangers still come and care and pray. A man from our church comes every Sunday morning and stays with Ricky and we go to church as a family."

She didn't want us to leave and we didn't want to, but our schedules demanded that we go. She smiled, "People are what keep me going—and God. When there's a need someone always responds. People keep on helping us with the little things and God keeps taking care of the big things."

My friend asked softly, "May we pray?"

"Oh, yes, back by Ricky's bed. It will upset him, but let's go back there."

We didn't understand, but she was determined, so we followed. Betty's shoulders straightened and she wiped away the tears.

"Ricky, shut your eyes, honey. We want to pray."

His sudden screams pierced the room. Big tears rolled from his eyes, dampening the pillow. He tried to struggle.

"No," we protested. "Please, let's don't upset him."

I pulled at Betty's arm trying to get her to leave the room. I wanted to get away from the screams.

Betty stood firm, explaining loudly over his cries, "Ricky screams every time someone prays for him. The doctors think he may be remembering his life before the accident and this remembering stimulates the brain. They encourage it."

In a softer voice, she reasoned, "I think Ricky is praying, too. He used to pray aloud every Sunday in his Sunday School class. Did I tell you that Ricky was saved a few months before the accident? I couldn't stand this if he weren't saved."

We bowed our heads and my friend prayed. Ricky screamed long and loud. His mother held onto him. I wanted to help but didn't know how, so I put my hand on her back. I felt her muscles getting tense.

Ricky's mother walked to the back door with us as we left. I noticed her Sunday School lesson book sandwiched in her worn Bible on a table. I remembered when I hadn't taken time to study my own.

"Thank you for coming," her face crumbled with these words.

I called Betty a few weeks later and she excitedly told me Ricky was eating baby food! The tube and catheter had been removed. "I put the big card you made on the ceiling over his bed. He wakes up looking at it."

"I'll make another one," I offered.

Muffled sobs came over the phone, then she said quickly

and clearly, "Thank you. This time, could you make a pony?"

"Oh, yes, of course," I replied eagerly, thinking to myself, "It's such a little thing to do." But instantly I remembered how happy Betty had looked when she told us, "People keep helping us with the little things and God is taking care of the big things."

(Editor's note: Ricky continues to make progress. In May 1974, fifteen months after the accident, he had his first speech therapy lesson and did say "Mama." By late 1974 he turned over by himself. In June 1975, following complicated surgery, Ricky began to eat real food. Betty Shadburn writes that she felt God reach down and nearly touch her, urging, "Hang on a little while longer, Betty.")

21
Something Special for Angela

"Mama," Jennifer sighed, "Angela's mother lets her do a lot of the cooking. Angela's mother teaches her how to do it."

"That's nice," I answered, not looking up, as I cracked an egg into my mixing bowl.

"Know something else?" Jennifer continued, as if I were really carrying on a conversation with her. "Her mother goes to the movies with her, even if it's a movie just for children."

"Uh-huh," I murmured, as I stirred the corn bread and glanced at the oven to be sure I had turned it on.

Jennifer started to say something else, but the phone rang. As I became involved in the phone conversation, she slipped out of the kitchen.

After that, though, I often heard about Angela and her mother, and one day Angela came home from school with Jennifer. I liked her right away. She was a slim child with a wonderful smile that seemed to explode quietly. She spoke softly and wasn't silly as many twelve-year-olds can be.

Later, when I drove Angela home, I went in to meet her mother. She was standing at the sink and she turned and flashed a smile at me just as bright as her daughter's. I felt welcomed. We chatted for a few minutes. She was the kind of person I wanted to know better.

Just before Christmas Jennifer told me that Angela's mother was in the hospital, but that she might be home for Christmas.

"Well, she probably will, I answered brightly. "I certainly hope so, anyway."

"She's having some treatments. Co . . . something. I can't remember the name," Jennifer said.

"Cobalt?" I asked, not even liking to say the word.

"Yes, that's it. What does it mean?"

Surely Jennifer's wrong, I thought. Twelve-year-olds often get things terribly mixed up.

Jennifer didn't wait for me to answer about the treatments, and I was grateful. Instead, she talked on some more about Angela's mother being sick.

Jennifer had been out of school several days with a virus so she and Angela had been out of touch. She talked about calling Angela to find out how her mother was, but decided to wait and see her at school the next day.

Just then my twin sons came in from school, both talking at once. "Mama, our bus patrol's mother died. Can we have money for flowers?"

Fear twisted in my heart. "Yes, of course. What was the matter with her?"

"She had cancer," one of the boys answered.

Jennifer spoke softly, "What is your bus patrol's name?"

"Um—John Michael."

"Mama," Jennifer whispered. "That's Angela's mother."

A call to the school confirmed that Angela's mother had died the day before.

"I have to go see Angela, Mama," Jennifer said softly. "Will you take me?"

"Of course," I answered.

We went by a shopping center on the way and Jennifer selected an arrangement of cactus plants in a dainty, handpainted dish. "She'll like this," Jennifer said, pleased with her purchase. But as we drove on to Angela's house, Jennifer's face clouded, "Mama, I don't know what to say to her."

"You'll know when you see her. Don't plan anything."

A relative answered the door and told us they were all out of town for the funeral. They would be back the day before Christmas Eve.

Jennifer didn't leave the cactus plants. "I'll bring it back," she told the man who had answered the door. He smiled and nodded.

The day before Christmas the phone rang and Jennifer answered it. "It's Angela," she whispered to me. "She wants me to come see her."

So we went back with the plants in hand. I was a bit startled to see that the front door had been gaily decorated. Angela greeted us with her radiant smile and welcomed us in. Her father wasn't at home, but she introduced us to her grandmother and grandfather. Her little brother played with a small truck and looked up at the Christmas tree often. It was large and tall, touching the ceiling. Stockings hung by the fireplace; a small nativity scene sat on a table.

Angela was pleased with the gift, touching it ever so gently with one finger. As Angela took Jennifer into the den to show her the Christmas tree, I sat at the kitchen table and talked with Angela's paternal grandparents. "Their mother suffered so much the last few months . . . so much," her grandfather told me. "The children knew how terribly she was suffering. Janet, Angela's mother, had known for eight years that she had cancer. She had expected to live only a short while."

Jennifer's words drifted through my mind with sudden clarity. "Angela's mother . . ."

Angela came home with us for the afternoon. I had a few errands to run and when I introduced Angela to one of my friends, she flashed that warm smile of hers. When my friend wished Jennifer and Angela a merry

Christmas, Jennifer looked at Angela uncertainly. But Angela answered for both of them with quiet enthusiasm. "Merry Christmas to you, too."

It seemed each time I glanced at Angela during the afternoon, she would smile quickly and reassuringly at me. When her daddy came to pick her up, she thanked us for having her over and wished us a very heartfelt merry Christmas. I watched her run to the car and join her father. They were going Christmas shopping.

Angela came back two days after Christmas and brought a knitted hanging basket to show us. She'd made it for the cactus plants. She also brought some bread that she had baked herself.

Her grandmother phoned and wanted to talk to her. I couldn't help overhearing part of the conversation. "You just pound the steak, Grandmother . . . and I know the way Daddy and John Michael like their gravy. Let me make it. I'll be home in a little bit."

As Angela thanked me for the afternoon, I brushed back a strand of her long hair. I wanted to squeeze her to me, but I didn't. Her father waved to me from the car and I waved back. We had met only once. Somehow I sensed this wasn't the time to speak to him or to offer my sympathy.

But I wanted to do more than offer my sympathy. I wanted to say to him, "You must be so proud of Angela."

Back in the kitchen, as I started supper, I thought about Angela. Making gravy, grocery shopping, knitting, cleaning the house, having a daddy and a little brother who could depend on her, wishing others a merry Christmas this year when she had suffered such a loss were just part of it. Angela's mother had taught her in twelve years what many of us never learn—how to live, how to go on living, fully, no matter how great the loss.

I saw her only once—just for a few moments—but I

knew I wanted to be more like Angela's mother, and I had to begin somewhere.

Jennifer came into the kitchen and stood close to me like a small shadow, watching me peel the potatoes.

I handed her the peeler and said, "I could sure use some help, Jen. How about making the mashed potatoes tonight?"

22
Not Really Alone

The minister of education at our church handed me a slip of paper and asked, "Will you go by and see her? She called the church for help. I've been; but a woman should visit with her. It involves a divorce." I took the scrap of paper, said I would be glad to go by, and stuck it in my sweater pocket. I didn't plan to go right away, but that piece of paper seemed to get heavier and heavier in my pocket. I woke up the next morning having already decided to go meet Rhyne Sommers.

I drove slowly down the unfamiliar street, admiring the beautifully manicured lawns and rustic mailboxes. Finally, a house number matched the number on the paper in my hand. I pulled into the driveway and smiled at the house. It welcomed me with country charm which included a deacon's bench and lots of hanging baskets. Flowers lined the rock walkway. I was nervous about meeting Rhyne. I had no idea how to help. Just before I rang the doorbell, I prayed, "Lord, I don't know anything about helping someone who's going through divorce." For a moment I nearly prayed that no one would answer the door. I took a deep breath and pushed the bell, once, twice.

It opened suddenly and a little girl about four looked up at me. She was such a beautiful child, the kind I had seen on the front of Mother Goose books, with long golden hair and inquisitive eyes, that for a moment I didn't say anything. I just stared at her.

"Hi," she broke the silence.

"Hi, is your Mama at home?"

"Yes." She turned around and called, "Maaamaaa . . ."

I stepped inside the door and felt comfortable in the warm friendly den. The child called her mother again and looked at me, seemingly a bit worried; a little tense. Her expression suddenly seemed much older than her few years. "Mama is coming," she reassured me.

Rhyne Sommers joined us. She made very little effort to smile or pretend that things were fine. She appeared ready to collapse. The little girl looked up at her mother gravely. Rhyne thanked me for coming, introduced herself and her little daughter, Emily. We left Emily watching television and went into the living room to talk.

I suspected that Rhyne wasn't the complaining type and that talking about herself was difficult. Sitting erect, her mouth grimly set, eyes puffy, she looked at me and then down at her hands, tightly clenched together. She seemed in such utter despair that I wanted to get up and run out the door. "Lord, help me. What do I say?"

Tell her about yourself—problems you've been through and how I was sufficient. Just talk about yourself for a while.

I began telling her about some rough experiences I had been through, feeling she absorbed every word. We looked at each other more and more as I spoke, slowly becoming friends. She nodded often, smiled a time or two, then began talking so softly that I had to strain to hear. "Right out of the blue, Richard told me that he wanted a divorce—wants to be free. I thought our marriage was wonderful," she said hoarsely. Tears spilled down her face and dampened her blouse.

"Asking for help of any kind is difficult for me," she almost smiled. It was my turn to nod. I understood that. Rhyne admitted that while she believed in God and had been in church almost all of her life, that now she needed something else—a more intense relationship with God. She added, "I guess I made Richard my god."

We talked for almost two hours and then went into the kitchen so she could write down my telephone number. I couldn't help admiring her gracious home and charming kitchen—even the way the sun shone into the kitchen through the spotless window and streamed across the shining floor seemed perfect to me.

Rhyne and I exchanged telephone numbers and while she wrote I thought of something that seemed like excellent advice, wise and scriptural. "Rhyne," I began almost glibly, confident my illustration would help her. Then she looked up at me and I noticed that her hand shook as she wrote. I saw the deep agony in her eyes—like a doomed animal in a trap. I didn't share my advice. We just looked at each other. Tears slid down her face and she made a great effort not to cry or lose control. A knot developed in my own throat, and the next moment we were in each other's arms, sobbing. No words were adequate. So we just cried together in her beautiful kitchen as the sun streamed in through the quaint kitchen window as though her world were not falling apart.

I called Rhyne the next day and we talked comfortably. She started coming to church and Sunday School regularly. We visited and talked on the phone often. Sometimes we prayed together, or shared Scripture. One Sunday we were sitting together in church and during the invitation hymn I stole a quick glance at her. I hadn't intended it, but our eyes met. She smiled, squeezed my hand quickly, and walked down the aisle. Rhyne was baptized that night and even with her pretty, short hair wet, she was beautiful. Something new shone in her blue eyes.

Rhyne's husband, Richard, still wanted his freedom.

That she loved him dearly was quite evident even when she spoke his name, but she agreed to the divorce. Mostly she didn't complain about her suffering. Then, she called one afternoon and was crying. "Oh, Marion, it hurts so bad. I don't think I can do it. I'm not going to be able to give him up. I can't. I just can't. Even if I give him the divorce, I can't let go of him in my heart."

Her defeat and despair came over the telephone and seemed to fill my kitchen. Rhyne was at her lowest. I suddenly believed that if she would take one small step of faith now that God would meet her deepest need. "Listen, Rhyne, will you come to prayer meeting to-night?" It was Wednesday and she had started coming to our regular midweek prayer service at church.

"No, I don't feel like coming."

"Please. Forget how you feel. Come, not just to be in the church, but just to make one move that you don't feel like making or even understand. Just trust God, please."

"I don't know."

"I'll be looking for you."

"I don't think I'm coming. You don't know how I feel."

We hung up and I prayed that God, who knew exactly how she felt, would get her there someway.

I sat on the back row at church praying she would come even though the service had started. I sat alone that evening. Announcements were made and we were singing. Finally, I heard the door open softly. I continued singing, joyfully. I just knew it would be Rhyne. She slid into the pew by me and put her hand under half the hymnbook that I held. She leaned over and said, with utter joy, "I believe!" Then we sang together, "Be not dismayed what 'er betide, God will take care of you . . ."

The next week Rhyne agreed to meet Richard at the lawyer's office to sign the final papers. She told me, "The

night before I was to sign the paper I got this tremendous
desire to make Richard his favorite fresh apple pie. I
know Jesus gave me the idea and helped me do it. I
made it with joy, just like nothing was wrong. I couldn't
have done that. When he came by the house I served
him fresh, hot apple pie. I don't understand it," Rhyne
marveled. Then, she continued, smiling, "And when I had
to drive to the lawyer's office, I was scared. There was
nobody to go with me. But I started singing 'Jesus Loves
Me,' and I didn't feel alone anymore!"

I stared in amazement. She laughed a little, "I can't
explain it. I just know Jesus is with me, all the way. He's
even keeping the bitterness away."

One morning she stopped by my house with some
homemade pumpkin bread. She wore a bright red sweater,
and her cheeks were flushed from the cold. She had a
smart new haircut and never seemed to stop smiling.
Looking at her, I thought, you've passed me in our spiritual walk. You're teaching me now. How grateful I am
to know you.

One night at church I asked Rhyne how she would
feel about my including her remarkable story as a chapter
in my new book. I was all ready for her to say no. I
would have understood. But her face lit up and tears
brimmed her bright eyes. "Oh, yes, please share my story.
Tell others who may be going through it. Tell women
who feel shame, who've had their pride crushed publicly,
that Jesus will get them through it. He will put them
back together again, and they don't have to be alone."

I nodded gratefully and we left the church. I watched
Rhyne come out of the nursery with Emily. It was a
dark night—no stars or moon. But I had the warmest
assurance that the one who loved Rhyne the most and
had healed her heart, climbed right into the car with
her and Emily and went home with them.

23
Peace Like a River

On the first few notes of the hymn of invitation, a young girl moved forward in our church at the Sunday evening service. As she spoke to the pastor, a grave expression crossed his face. Usually our minister's face doesn't reveal the nature of whatever people share with him during the invitation. But this time, it became obvious that he was deeply shocked.

We stopped singing and Dr. Bagwell shared with us what he had been told. A sudden flood had hit a section of Colorado. People were missing and assumed dead. A couple and their children from our church were attending the annual training session for Campus Crusade for Christ International in Ft. Collins, Colorado—right where the monster flood raged.

"Charles and Dawn and their children are all right," the pastor quickly assured us, "but seven women with Campus Crusade are missing."

A low moan spread through the church. We stood motionless for a moment then bowed for prayer. Dr. Bagwell had difficulty expressing his prayer, but finally prayed audibly and hesitantly. In our hearts, we prayed silently.

Leaving the church I thought, surely now the others with Campus Crusade must turn back and come home. Their meetings have just begun, but they will, of course, come home. How can they go on after this tragedy?

Within the next few days the bodies of the seven young

girls along with other victims were recovered. The papers carried accounts of how their backs and necks had been snapped in two by the incredibly swift water. Identification was difficult because the water had torn off almost all clothing, and even jewelry. Bodies were found fifteen miles from where they had been at the time the roaring wall of water swept down on the trapped people.

The Campus Crusade people had not, however, come home.

When Dawn got back to Atlanta she called me. Her voice sounded bright, as usual. She told me that thirty of the women in leadership positions with their group, along with Dr. Bill Bright's wife, Vonette, had gone to a separate place to pray. Suddenly they heard loud-speakers booming. Without any other warning, they were urged to leave immediately. At first the women thought it was some kind of a joke. But then they quickly realized differently, and piled into cars, not sure which way to head. Some of them went one way—others, another way. It was dark and mass confusion prevailed.

Dawn told me about a girl from Atlanta, Melanie Alquist.

Later I got to hear her amazing testimony in person and on television. The car she had chosen to escape in suddenly left the road and bobbled in the raging river for a moment.

When I heard Melanie share her experience, she had smiled at this point and explained, "All of us in the car were praying—but our prayers weren't panicky. We were thanking Jesus for seeing us, for knowing exactly what was happening. No one screamed. All I heard were soft murmurings of 'Thank You, Jesus.' Somehow I got out through a window. I fully expected to drown and sort of waited to see if my life would flash by me in those last few moments. It didn't. I thought for an instant about my family. But then I thought, any second now, I'll be with Jesus.

"Then I hit a calm spot in the water and was able to catch my breath and see. Those few moments of being in almost still water enabled me to spot a tree just ahead. Almost gently, the water took me to the tree and I grabbed on. Debris nearly pinned me to the tree then gradually piled up underneath me and provided a ladder.

"*Thank You, Lord.*" I prayed joyfully.

"The waters continued to rise and I moved to the top of the tree. Even in the darkness I could make out the bank about a half a block away. Suddenly I saw a man and began to call out to him, 'Help!'

"Then, I realized that even though I'd lost my clothes and jewelry, the one thing I really needed, God had allowed me to keep. I still wore my contact lenses! Without them I could have never seen the man on the shore.

"The man called back to me, and after a while I saw lights over on the bank—car lights. Perhaps five or six pairs appeared. I had never seen such beautiful lights in my life.

"I suddenly realized that many people are living in spiritual darkness and desperately need light. I made a mental recommitment to God. If I lived through the flood, I wanted to spend the rest of my life helping those in darkness to see the light of the world—Jesus."

Melanie told us how she sat behind branches in the tree without any clothes and watched two young men making their way to rescue her. The man on the bank had found two men, highly skilled in this type of rescue. Finally one of the men made his way to the tree, looked up, and called out, "Hi, my name's Paul and we're going to get you out of here."

Melanie responded gratefully by easing herself down the tree.

Paul and Scott got Melanie to the shore by holding onto a rope. Once on dry land, she collapsed.

Melanie and one other girl were the only survivors in the car she had selected to ride in.

Dawn told me that while the search for bodies continued the next day, many of the Campus Crusade members prayed, shared Scripture and sang. She said that somehow the songs that were sung the most were about water. "On Jordan's stormy banks I stand" "Peace like a mighty river" "floods of joy o'er my soul like the sea billows roll, since Jesus came into my heart" "Like a river glorious is God's perfect peace."

Through talking to Dawn and hearing Melanie share, I came to realize that the girls who died were, like Melanie, ready to meet Jesus. They could live for him or die for him—it didn't make much difference.

I thought a lot about the girls and their families. Our local newspaper, *The Atlanta Journal*, carried a full page memorial to the girls, including their pictures. The memorial explained the plan of salvation in simple terms. The bold letters above the memorial said, "These women lost their lives in the Colorado flood, but they are still alive. They have a message for you."

I read later in the *National Courier* an article by Vonette Bright. She stated that one hundred fifty million people read that ad as it was picked up by newspapers all over the country. In her article she also stated that as many as five million people could have made commitments to Christ as a result of the message.

Melanie now spends her time going to schools, colleges, churches—anywhere there are people—to share her testimony and explain to people how to invite Jesus into their hearts.

One of the girls who was killed had made the statement to many of her friends, "I would give anything—anything—if members of my family would come to know Jesus." The family members she had been praying for turned their lives over to Jesus after her funeral.

I put the memorial to the seven girls on my kitchen bulletin board. As I tacked it up, I noticed that the corner of it touched my daily devotional calendar, and I read the message of the day. "August 17, 1976—Tuesday— Fear not . . . when thou passeth through the waters, I will be with thee; and through the rivers, they shall not overflow thee" (Isa. 43:1-2, KJV).

I've thought about those young girls and wondered if they could have known somehow what the trip to Colorado would cost them—wouldn't they have gone ahead anyway?

PART FIVE—THE NITTY-GRITTY

Not one sparrow . . . can fall to the ground without your Father knowing it (Matt. 10:29).

24
Lifting My Head from the Sand

I was in my late twenties when I really began to think about Franklin D. Roosevelt's statement, "The only thing we have to fear is fear itself" (First Inaugural Address, March 4, 1933).

Right, I agreed. But being afraid of being afraid is still something I can't cope with.

Often I didn't even know what I was afraid of. Struggling in a quicksand of fear, I decided, it doesn't matter what it is . . . I'm afraid of it. I used to awaken in the middle of the night with my heart pounding in a gripping fear as I thought about facing the next day. There would be decisions to make and people's opinions of my decisions to consider. Perhaps most frightening of all there would be inevitable failures.

Wouldn't it be just wonderful to pull the covers over my head, like an ostrich in the sand and not face any of it, anymore. Yes, yes, Satan urged. Do just that!

Once when my oldest daughter was three and a half, her grandmother took her for a walk. An airplane roared overhead and Julie lifted her face upward. She stopped walking and a frozen look of fear crossed her face. "Goge, (Go'-ge—her name for my mother) don't let dat big fence fall on me." Julie put her hands up protectively over her head.

My mother glanced up puzzled and finally understood. Julie had noticed for the first time power and telephone poles with wires stretched from one to the other. To her it could be only one thing—a tremendous fence that didn't look too sturdy.

Julie's grandmother picked her up and held her close. Then she explained exactly what the poles deeply set in the ground were for. She explained that Julie talked to her through those wires when she called on the phone. A relieved smile came over my daughter's face. As they continued their walk, Julie glanced upward often and smiled at the poles and wires confidently.

When our twins were kindergarten age we were attending church one evening and the pastor announced, "Those families wishing to do so, please come forward and kneel at the altar for Jesus' sake." Our family moved forward. Jeremy came holding my hand, but as we knelt I noticed he was sobbing softly and shaking.

"What's wrong," I whispered. But he only shook his head and cried harder. He covered his mouth with his hand, trying to muffle his sobs. He was obviously frightened of something. He loved the church, the pastor, and Jesus. I didn't understand. On the way home, my husband, the other children, and I tried to persuade him to tell us what was wrong. But he shook his head and remained silent.

Finally, as I put him to bed, I insisted that he tell me why he was afraid.

"Well," he said, "I was scared of getting nailed."

"Of what," I exclaimed.

"The preacher said to come get nailed for Jesus sake and I thought they was 'gonna nail me to the wall."

"Oh, no, Jeremy. He said kneel. Do you know what that is?"

Still not smiling, he shook his head.

I got down on my knees and said, "See, I'm kneeling. This is my knee."

A tremendous smile covered his face and he suddenly

sat erect on his bunk bed, swinging his feet happily, and sighed, "Oh."

Two years later Jeremy came screaming into the house one afternoon. All I could understand him say was dog. He screamed so loudly and was so frightened, I assumed he had been bitten.

"Where did he bite you," I cried, examining him.

"He didn't," he hollered, still jumping up and down and pointing to the door.

"What's the matter, then?" I was screaming now. Fear is contagious.

"The dog . . . the dog . . ." he cried over and over.

"Come on. Let's go see the dog," I grabbed his hand.

"No," he pulled back.

"What's the matter with the dog?"

"He scares me," he wailed loudly.

"How," I asked, knowing how much he loved dogs.

"He's . . . he's . . . he's just got . . . three . . . legs. Waaaahhh."

"Come on, show me."

Holding hands tightly, we walked out into the yard together. A beautiful collie galloped by on three legs. His left hind leg had been amputated up to the hip. The dog wagged his tail at us. He was well cared for and a healthy dog. The fur was just beginning to grow back where the vet had shaved him for surgery.

"Jeremy, isn't that wonderful," I exclaimed, smiling.

He looked at my smile in a puzzled way, "Huh?"

"Someone loved their dog so much they took him to the vet who must have saved his life. And God gave dogs four legs. See, he can manage quite well. See how he gets around and plays with the other dogs. They don't seem to notice he's different. Why, this is like a miracle. I'm so glad you showed this beautiful dog to me. I feel good about him."

The dog came toward us and I knelt down by Jeremy and whistled. Jeremy had stopped crying, but hung back. The dog came up and licked my hand and I petted him. Slowly Jeremy reached toward the dog. It suddenly licked him in the face and Jeremy grabbed the collie around the neck in a bear hug. Then they tumbled together in the grass and Jeremy laughed aloud.

When Jeremy's father came home that evening Jeremy got to him first. "Daddy, we saw a dog today and it was wonderful! The vet took his leg off and he's just fine now. I like him. No reason to be scared of a dog with three legs." Since then I've thought if I would go to my Father and confess my fears openly to him, he would take me by the hand like a loving parent and calm me by saying something like, *"Let's go a bit closer. Things don't look so frightening when you get closer and understand. Maybe you've misunderstood, child. Come, stand close to me and let's look at this thing together."*

He often speaks to me softly like this, but I'm whimpering so loudly that I don't pay any attention to his soothing explanation.

I just continue in my fear.

"Get your head out of the sand, Marion. Look up. Come on with me. I'll walk by your side. Come on," he encourages.

When I finally lift my head up, stop my bellowing, and go with him, my fears are dissolved. Often I discover something quite wonderful, instead of fearful. Sometimes, though, it has taken years for me to move forward past a certain fear. The hardest part is pulling my head from the sand and moving ahead again, refusing to be stopped or turned back by the fear monster.

25
Who Me, Teach?

I hid my fear of speaking or teaching way back in a dark, secret place in my heart and nourished it privately. The fear grew rapidly to enormous proportions.

Each year I made the same curt speech to the nominating committee in our church about how I hadn't been called to teach. I had gotten so I could say my speech without batting an eye and almost without feeling anything deep inside me.

I had seven good reasons why I couldn't and shouldn't accept a teaching position. I kept reminding God and the nominating committee of them. Still, I flinched, almost involuntarily, when anyone mentioned the great need for Sunday School teachers.

"I can't Lord. You know I can't. I'm too frightened to speak in front of anyone. My mouth gets dry and my voice trembles. My mind's a total blank. I don't understand the Bible and can't pronounce half the names in it. Please, understand, Lord."

For two years I told him and the committee, no. It got harder and harder. What if God was calling me to teach. Sometimes I felt certain he was. Maybe he will change his mind, I hoped. Or, if I go ahead and teach and fall on my face, he will surely say, "Well, you tried, Marion. You really can't teach."

The first time I knew for certain he meant for me to teach was when I had been asked to draw and tell a story to second graders for Bible School. I sat alone in our recreation room making drawings to illustrate the story and saying the story aloud to myself as I drew. And I prayed. I prepared for the little story as though it were a baccalaureate address.

As I sat crosslegged in the floor mumbling to myself and drawing furiously, one by one my children drifted in to watch me and ask questions. Finally, Julie said, "Mama, tell us the story like we are your Bible School children. Practice on us."

For a moment I felt the old, familiar fear spring up and thought, goodness, I can't even do this in front of my own children. But because I felt so ridiculous saying no, I said, "OK." They lined up against the wall.

As I began telling the story using my drawings I realized that I really had their attention. Something quite rare. My children seldom listened to me lecture about anything. Toward the end of the story I saw a tear slide down Jennifer's face. One of the boys sobbed out loud. Tears rapidly filled Julie's eyes. My own vision blurred. Before I finished a sweet presence seemed to fill the room and a joy burst forth in my heart. As I was teaching, I was being taught. I knew right then that God intended me to teach.

But that night I put that experience and the knowledge that I received out of my mind. I chalked it up as an unforgettable sharing time between mother and children.

A year later a friend and I went to visit a young mother whom we thought was on the verge of accepting Christ. Her two young daughters were so loud and demanding that I finally suggested taking them out in the backyard and letting my friend talk to the mother about Jesus. As the children and I went out the back door I thought, why did I have to get stuck with the children? I wanted to be the one to share Jesus with the mother.

The sun shone hotly out back even though it was still

early morning. I suggested we sit under the only tree in the yard, a large oak. An inner tube hung from a rope attached to a bent limb of the tree. The lack of grass underneath it indicated that the girls often played there. We trudged through the tall grass and weeds, still wet with dew. I sat on a big rock and Rachel immediately gathered several small stones and fashioned herself a chair similar to mine. Karen, her handicapped sister, stood by, not sure exactly what to do.

"I'll tell you a story one at a time. One of you swing, while I tell the other a story and in a few minutes, we'll swap." Karen nodded and headed stiffly for the swing while Rachel, the younger child, wrapped her arms around her knees anticipating the story.

I told her stories about Jesus. We sang simple songs about him. Suddenly, I realized, *I'm having fun!* The thought so startled me that I stopped singing, grinning to myself.

"Sing, West," Rachel urged, smiling.

I felt God with us in a special way and prayed, "Thank you, Lord, for sending me out here with these children and for this joy."

In a few minutes I announced, "Time to change places." The girls immediately changed places and I watched Rachel's attempt to get her short leg up in the inner tube.

"Lord, please help Rachel. I'm going to suggest something and I'll need your help."

"West, help me," Rachel called out.

"Rachel, who were we just talking about?"

"Jesus."

"And what did I tell you about him?"

"He loves me."

"What else?"

"He will help me."

"Would you like to ask him to help you right now?"

A tremendous grin spread over her face. She threw her head back, looked up at the blue sky calling out loudly, "Jesus, I need you to help me get in this swing. I never got in it by myself before. Help me." She swung her foot up again and again. On the third try it landed in the inner tube and slowly she pulled herself up.

"Thank you, Lord," I breathed.

"West, he did it! He did it! I never got up by myself before."

"As Rachel continued swinging and singing her own version of Jesus loves Rachel, I told Karen about Jesus.

Finally, Rachel was at the swing again. "Jesus, I need you to help me again." She huffed a bit, but swung her foot all the way up calling to me, "He did it again, West."

"Yes," I thought, "he's done it again for me, too. I love teaching."

But I still wouldn't give in. The nominating committee was meeting again. My husband was a member this year and he told me of the difficulty in getting teachers for Sunday School. Many had said, "Well, if you just can't get anyone else . . . ."

"What kind of attitude is that for a teacher," I stormed. "Teachers should have joy and accept a position with enthusiasm."

Jerry looked at me silently and I slunk away. Later that week I got out his teacher's book and the Bible when no one was at home except me and secretly prepared a lesson, pretending I was a teacher. It was fun.

I loved my own Sunday School class. It was special and one of the reasons I had for not teaching. I couldn't leave my class. But I was getting tired of explaining these seven reasons over and over to God and the committee. "Lord, if you're calling me to teach, let someone call and ask me to substitute. No one has ever asked me to

do that." That week a departmental superintendent called
to ask if I could teach his wife's class for two weeks.
They would be out of town. I stammered, refused, and
practically threw the phone down.

Then I called him back and accepted with great fear.
For the two weeks before I was to teach I studied and
prayed and made notes. I loved preparing the lesson, but
I became so frightened when I entered the classroom
that Sunday morning that I thought about running and
hiding in the car. The young girls drifted in. Their smiles
lifted my fears some. I told them I was scared to death
and had never taught. They smiled even more and gave
me their undivided attention. I began speaking. We had
prayer and I asked the Holy Spirit to teach the lesson.
I heard my voice, even saw myself using my hands as
I spoke, but I felt as though I were over in a corner
watching. I thought, Lord, after this sentence, I don't
know what's coming. But the words continued to flow.
It was one of the most trusting experiences I have ever
been through. Another amazing thing happened, the bell
rang just as I finished.

The girls left and I sat alone for a few minutes thanking
God for holding me up. Then I went to church and cried
through the service because I was so happy.

I was asked to substitute quite a bit during the summer
and I accepted each opportunity and taught several age
groups. The fear came with each acceptance, but so did
God's assurance that he would help me.

Toward the end of the summer, I told Jerry, "I want
to talk to you."

"Something wrong?" he picked up the serious tone in
my voice.

"No, I'm just telling you, officially, as a member of
the nominating committee, that I'm volunteering to teach
wherever I'm needed."

"You're sure?" His mouth looked uncertain, but his eyes twinkled and encouraged me.

I nodded. "Just give me a class."

I was given the group of ninth grade girls I had taught on the first Sunday when I substituted. I left my own class and God gave me such a joy that I couldn't look back. I just couldn't.

I guess I grew more than any of the girls. They shared prayer requests with me, prayed for me, understood my fear of teaching. God instructed me not to make the gospel comfortable for them. Often I was tempted. But the whole year I stressed total surrender. "Lord, I must sound like a broken record, I keep saying the same thing!"

Toward the end of the year, I asked the Lord to let me know if any of them understood about selling out to Jesus, completely.

One Sunday I didn't want the class to be over. I felt certain that someone wanted to talk to me—make a decision. But the girls filed out. I left while two of them were gathering up their things. I was outside the building and at the top of the steps when I heard one of them call, "Mrs. West, come back!"

Joy exploded in my heart and I knew. Oh, I knew what they wanted. I jumped down the steps three at a time and ran back into the room. Tears streamed down their faces. I started crying. We sat down together, holding hands. Then we laughed and wiped each other's mascara with a tissue.

"We want to make Jesus Lord," one of them said. "I'm scared. It means a whole new way of life. But I want to do it."

"Me, too," the other one said.

Two of the most honest prayers I've ever been privileged to hear were prayed in that room and we went into the church services holding hands. During the invitation the two girls made their decisions public and I thought surely I would faint from happiness.

Like Jeremy who in fear reached out to a three-legged dog because I asked him to, I moved forward into a teaching position and discovered, like my child had, something quite wonderful and thrilling. "Oh, Lord, thank you for this experience, for these girls, for not letting me run away from teaching. What do you want me to do next?"

26
I Am Weak, but He Is Strong

This chapter isn't for everyone. It is for people who are ridiculously involved with animals beyond the point of all reason. My apologies to those who don't understand.

Early in life I knew I was one of those people who wasn't going to be reasonable about animals. Too late my husband discovered it. I'm the only mother on our street who brings home stray animals. Other mothers call me when a bird falls out of a tree, a dog is hit by a car, or a stray, hungry cat or dog appears in the neighborhood.

Right after our first child was born we decided to get a dog. We selected a runt of a litter of eleven puppies. We took the little black dog because no one else wanted her.

Muff caused years of confusion and apologies. She dug up the yard, tore down screen doors when it thundered, pulled sheets off clothes lines, barked at nothing for hours, and raided our neighbor's garbage can. Part bird dog and part setter, she assumed she was like us, human.

When she reached the age of fourteen, she began to settle down a bit and I told Jerry, "See, I told you she would grow out of those bad habits. Actually, she was becoming feeble. Her hearing was affected, but she could still "feel" thunder. She had severe kidney problems, arthritis, cataracts, infected teeth, and she finally lost control of her bowels. But her heart was amazingly strong, the vet said. By the time she reached fifteen we talked about having her put to sleep.

Several times when Jerry took her to the vet with a new ailment I resigned myself to the fact that he could return without Muff. But each time he would get out of the car and I would watch him go around to the other side and open the door, my heart would beat wildly with gratitude, and I would think, not this time. Muff would lumber out of the car, almost in slow motion, and look at me with her strange lopsided grin and wag her sparsely furred tail. Her hair had begun to come out, too. A giant wart on the end of her nose, the size of a little finger, wobbled as she walked.

Sometimes the children and I went with Jerry when he took Muff to the vet. It was then that I realized fully how decrepit she had become. As frisky pups, pedigree dogs, or even young mutts obeyed commands of "Sit," Muff would inevitably collapse in the vet's waiting room on the slippery floor.

That is, once we got her into his office. Jerry would pull her gently through the door. I would push from behind so that we would slide her across the floor as though she were a statue. We learned to ignore the stares and comments of people waiting with their pets.

Once an elderly lady holding her miniature dog asked, "What's that on your dog's nose?" Jerry, who's usually extremely polite to little, old ladies, answered without batting an eye, "Another nose."

Fortunately, she was hard of hearing and asked again. Quickly, I explained about the wart that was continuing to grow. Muff lay sprawled in the middle of the floor like a newborn deer. She had an abcessed tooth that day and her face was swollen. She drooled like a mad dog. Everyone picked up their pet and looked at us with disapproval.

The vet gave her a shot and made another appointment.

I took her back for the appointment. It was an hour's drive. We still took her back from Atlanta to Athens, Georgia, where we had formerly lived. We just knew that Dr. Causey understood Muff.

Driving over to Athens, Muff tried to get up on the seat by me, where she usually rode. She fell backwards and decided not to try again. Every movement was a tremendous effort for her. I glanced down at the old dog and a look seemed to cross her face—I've had it. I can't go on.

Lord, I prayed, if it's time for Muff to be put to sleep, let Dr. Causey suggest it as soon as I see him. I'm not going to say anything, and I don't want him to beat around the bush. I can't take that.

Then I thought, but I can't do this. Jerry has promised that he would do it. Not me. I lifted my foot from the gas contemplating turning around and going back to Atlanta. Cars passed me and looked annoyed at my slow speed. "I can't, Lord. I'm too weak. I just can't do it."

Part of a song came to my mind, "I am weak, but Thou are strong, Jesus keep me from all wrong." Then the powerful thought: it's wrong to keep this animal living because of my weakness.

God seemed to guide me to pray for others then. I put my foot back on the gas and began praying for a friend who was having surgery right then; the girls I taught in Sunday school; people I knew with specific needs; a home about to break up; my children at school; Jerry at work; my ugly attitude about certain people. I prayed for about thirty minutes.

Then we were at the vet's. There wasn't anyone else in the waiting room. I had never seen Dr. Causey's office empty before. This must be for me, I thought. It will be easier without people watching me. Muff tried to climb up on my lap. She fell backwards onto the floor. I helped her up and she began pacing. She walked back into an examining room and Dr. Causey walked in after her. I followed. Dr. Causey's eyes met mine and he said without even examining Muff, "As a doctor, I can no longer recommend treating this dog. All her dignity is gone. Let her go. She's in a world of her own and confused—in pain. She's not your companion any more."

I thought slowly, I can do all things through Christ—all things—no exceptions. I don't have to be strong. He will be strong for me.

"How will you do it, Dr. Causey?"

"Instantly. All she will feel is the needle going in. There are many ways to do this. I will do it only one way. It will be over in five seconds. I had to do the same thing to my little dog. I helped her get into the world, and I helped her leave." Then he smiled at me.

"Can I stay with her?"

"If you want to."

He left the room for a moment and I looked at the white wall, refusing to let my eyes glance down at Muff. When the doctor came back in with the needle and an assistant, I knew I couldn't stay. Without touching Muff or looking at her, I walked quickly out the door and shut it gently. I looked out the window at a tree and tried to muffle my sobs. In just a few seconds Dr. Causey came out, still smiling, just a bit.

"Is she gone?"

He nodded and suggested I go into his office for a few minutes before driving. But I shook my head, I wanted to leave. "Thank you," I managed.

Back in the car I looked at the spot where Muff always rode. The car still smelled of her. I drove off sobbing and saying her name over and over aloud.

The Lord reminded me to praise him.

"Thank you, Lord, for Dr. Causey—he was so gentle

with Muff—and me. Thank you that he smiled at me. Thank you for the fifteen years we had Muff—all the trouble she caused, and all the pleasure she gave us. Thank you for being sufficient in all situations. Thank you because it is finally over for her."

You forgot to thank me for something, came the thought.

"Oh, Lord, I know what it is! I remembered the phone call that had come last night. Julie's boyfriend had called to ask if he could give her an early Christmas present—a baby kitten.

For fifteen years we had a rule at our house. No more pets as long as we had Muff and a cat, Wingate. But when I told Jerry what the call was about, with my hand over the phone, he smiled and said, "OK." I couldn't believe he had said yes, but I spoke into the receiver, "It's OK. You can bring the kitten over tomorrow."

"Thanks," the excited young boy said, "Don't tell Julie. It's a surprise."

Only God could have known the timing would be so perfect for us to have another pet on November 6, 1975. "Thank you, Lord, for the kitten we are going to get tonight. It'll be fun to have a new kitten." A tiny spark of joy ignited in my aching heart.

Everyone adjusted to the news about Muff pretty well. Jeremy began writing a story entitled, "The Day My Dog Died."

I answered the doorbell and was the first one to see our new kitty. She fit into the palm of Julie's boyfriend's hand. We went into the den and at first no one saw her because she was so small. Then Julie squealed with delight and reached out for the kitten. I saw tears glisten for a moment in her eyes as she tucked her head and made an effort not to cry.

God's timing is perfect—so is his strength.

27
The Joy of Belonging

I looked out of my kitchen window at the old house behind ours. The elderly couple who had lived there for many years had died within a year of each other. Their children and grandchildren had gathered, grieved, and gone.

The house is absolutely deserted, I thought.

Then I saw the two white cats. They made their way up the back steps to sit in the sun on the back porch. Their favorite overstuffed chair was gone. Everything was gone. Even from my kitchen window I could see they were pitifully thin. So, I thought, no one is going to claim the cats. They've been left to starve. They'll never leave that old place, I thought. They're shy, as their owners were.

They've never even been inside a house. Even during bitter cold winters they lived outside. Once, when the female cat had kittens, a dog killed them. After that the mama cat had her kittens in the attic of the one-hundred-year-old house, entering through a hole in the tin roof. Several times the kittens fell down into the small space between the walls. Once my neighbor told me, "We worked most all afternoon, but we finally got the kittens out. They would have starved to death."

When the kittens were brought outdoors, by their mother, they were thin, runny-eyed and frightened of anything that moved. They never played or even chased the mother cat's tail. I decided the other cat, a white male, was probably the female cat's son as well as the father of the kittens. Both were solid white, as were all the kittens.

I sighed, looking at the hungry cats sitting on the back porch. A familiar battle began inside me. Part of me wanted desperately to run to the cats. Another part of me wanted to turn away and never look at the starving cats again. It was frustrating to be a forty-year-old mother and still want to pick up stray animals. When I reached twenty-five, then thirty, then surely by thirty-five, I had assumed I would outgrow my obsession with abandoned animals. Now, I knew that it was only becoming worse with the years. When my husband reads in the paper about some little, old woman who lives alone with a hundred cats or so, he shows me the article and cautions, "Better watch out. You'll end up like this." It is typical of my obsession that I grab the article and read every word, then stare at the picture, usually of a thin, determined woman wearing tennis shoes and surrounded by cats who seem to be smiling and well fed. I love her!

There were no smiles on the forlorn cats who sat on the back porch of the abandoned house. I wiped my hands on my apron, grabbed two packages of cat food and headed for the old house. The cats darted beneath the porch as I approached. I crawled part of the way under the house that sat on concrete blocks and called, "Here kitties." I saw four slanted, bright eyes gleaming at me. It would be a long time before I could get close to them.

For several months I fed the cats this way. One day the mother cat came cautiously toward me and rubbed her face against my hand for a brief moment; then fear sprang into her eyes and she darted away. But after that she met me at the fence at five each day. The other cat would scamper away and hide in the bushes waiting for me to leave. I always talked to them as I put out

their food, calling them by the names I had given them—
Mama and Brother.

One day as Mama rubbed slowly against my leg with
her eyes almost shut in contentment, she purred for the
first time. My hand didn't reach out, not yet, but my
heart did. After that she often rubbed against me and
allowed me to stroke her—even before she touched the
food. Brother, reluctantly and stiff-necked, allowed me
to touch him occasionally; but he always endured my
affection, never received.

The cats grew fat. As I sat writing at my typewriter
one day, I saw Mama kitty on my patio. "Mama kitty,"
I whispered. She had never come into my yard before.
My own cats would never permit that—and yet, here
she was. "Good for you, Mama," I said to myself. Suddenly, she leaped up into the air and I thought for a
moment that she was choking. Then she seemed to be
chasing an object rapidly across the patio. Mama kitty
was playing for perhaps the first time in her life. I stopped
typing to watch her toss an acorn into the air and leap
after it. My cats came lurking toward the patio door to
try to hiss Mama kitty away. She only looked at them,
and continued playing with the acorn in the sun. Brother
sat on the fence, waiting for supper.

That summer Mama kitty had kittens again—in the
attic. She came to my back door to get me. I went with
her and crawled somewhat reluctantly into the dark attic,
ignoring the spiders, dust, heat, and rattling sounds that
I suspected were mice. Finally, I located the three kittens.
Brother stood guard over them.

I brought the kittens down and fixed a box for them
in the empty front bedroom of the old house. Mama kitty
wasn't too content with my moving her kittens, but she
let them stay—for awhile, anyway. Unexpectedly another
family moved into the house. Their moving frightened

Mama kitty and she returned her kittens to the only safety she knew—the dark, terribly hot attic.

I quickly explained to the family who had moved in about Mama kitty. They gave me permission to go into their attic and rescue the kittens. But I discovered Mama kitty had moved them to another spot. The old attic was a maze of hiding places. I couldn't find them.

Three times I went back to look, apologizing to the new tenants each time. Back at home, I would look out my window at the tin roof of the house. I could see the heat rising off it. The outside temperature stood in the upper nineties. The kittens couldn't possibly survive, and they would be wild if they did. I prayed, I cried, I fumed, and my last hope of saving the kittens seemed to shrivel up and die.

Then I happened to read a book that night that spoke to me about my rights as a child of God, *How to Live Like a King's Kid* by Harold Hill. The next morning before I opened my eyes I prayed, "Lord, I'm one of your children. I'm asking you to get me those kittens out of that attic. I can't find them. I don't see how you can get them out. But just please do it. If you don't they're going to die. In the name of Jesus and through his power, give me the kittens."

Silly maybe, but it didn't feel silly to an animal lover like myself. I hopped from the bed and ran to the back door, half expecting to find the kittens there. They weren't there—no sign of Mama or Brother either. Nevertheless, I expected to get the kittens.

My tolerant husband suggested that I go over one last time to look for them. The wife said, without enthusiasm, that I could go up in the attic again. Once I got up there I heard them meowing. "I'm coming. I'm coming," I called out, my heart pounding with joy.

The next moment I couldn't figure out what had happened. I seemed to be falling. Plaster broke loose. I wasn't in the dark, hot attic any more, but dangling into the kitchen. I had forgotten to stay on the rafters and had crashed through the ceiling. I climbed back up onto a rafter only to fall through again in another place.

Thoroughly shaken, I climbed back down. In the kitchen my neighbor and I looked at the damage. I grabbed her broom and began sweeping. More plaster fell on us and we coughed in the dust. I apologized over and over, babbling that we would have the ceiling fixed. I assured her I would be back over to talk with her husband. She nodded, silently, with her arms folded, and stared at me with seeming disbelief. I hurried home, humiliated, like a child who had gotten into trouble.

When I told Jerry and the children that night at supper, they all stared at me silently, like my new neighbor had. I was close to tears, partly because of the plight of the kittens, and for my own stupidity.

Jerry said, "I want you to go back tomorrow and speak to the husband. Offer to have the ceiling fixed and promise them both that you will never again go in their attic."

I nodded and looked so sad that Jerry softened his voice and asked, "Want me to go with you?"

I shook my head.

I arrived the next day during a meal. The couple's children were eating with them. They all stared at me as they continued eating. I was introduced as, "That woman who goes up in the attic all the time and fell through yesterday." I smiled at them all. The husband looked up at me, still chewing, and said solemnly, "Get my gun, Maw." For one horrible moment, my heart froze. Then he broke into a little-boy grin and continued, "Forget it. I'm a carpenter and the ceiling needed repairing, anyway."

I smiled back at him and added, "My husband said

to tell you that I wouldn't be going in your attic any more—ever."

"OK," he grinned, and I thought I heard his wife sigh.

The next afternoon, Sunday, our family sat in the living room reading the newspaper. Only I wasn't reading, I was praying behind my part of the paper. "Lord, it seems more hopeless than ever now. But I have no intention of giving up on this request. Give me the kittens, please. Thank you that I fell through the attic."

I have had some fantastic answers to prayer through praises—especially in bad situations, so I continued to praise God for the impossible situation. As I did, I imagined the kittens in a dark, obscure corner of the attic. I knew almost for certain that Mama kitty had moved them again. Then I imagined a large, gentle hand lifting them up and bringing them down into light and cooler air. I saw it in my mind, over and over, as I prayed. Suddenly, it seemed I could actually hear the kittens' tiny, helpless mews.

Silly, I told myself, your imagination goes wild when you pray.

Jerry put down the sports page; Jon and Jeremy looked up from the comics and the girls dropped their papers to their laps. We all listened quietly, almost without breathing. "Mew, mew, mew." It was real!

The doorbell rang and we all ran for it. I got there first and there stood my neighbor, cobwebs in his hair, dust on his overalls, and the impish little-boy grin on his lean face. We all looked down and there cradled in his hands were the kittens. "Lady, you won't have to look any more for 'em. I found 'em for you."

This time Mama kitty let her brood stay where I put them, in our small storeroom, just off the carport. We found excellent, cat-loving homes for the fat, playful kittens. And I found a permanent solution to the attic/kittens problem. I had Mama kitty spayed. God even provided the money. I had gotten an unexpected check, just the amount needed, from an article I had written that was reprinted.

Mama kitty had looked wildly at me as I drove her to the vet's. She had never been in a car before. Open fear shown in her eyes when I placed her in a cage near barking dogs. She shivered with terror. I stroked her through the cage and talked to her and I asked God to calm her. "This is the only way, Mama kitty. We can't go through that attic bit anymore." She licked my hand through the cage and began to purr.

Now Mama kitty comes right into the kitchen to eat from my other two cats' dish! She rubs against my leg when I let her in. On cold nights she sleeps curled up in a kitchen chair. And often she sits and watches me type. My cats hissed, growled, and fumed. Then, finally, they just gave up and accepted Mama kitty. I guess they realized that she had discovered the joy of belonging. I know how she feels. I can still remember the day I fully understood that I belonged to the family of God—I had been adopted!

Poor Brother—I know how he feels, too. He still sits cautiously on my backyard fence, cold, and often hungry. I sat on a fence, too, for years, skeptical about receiving unconditional love.

28
Praying About Orange Juice Cans

I answered the phone and could tell by the cheerful way the stranger on the other end said, "Mrs. West?" that she wanted me to do something. I decided right then I didn't want to do whatever it was she wanted help with. I was already too busy. I didn't have any extra time and effort to give her.

"Do you know about the Christmas store at the school?"

"Yes, I got the letter," I answered flatly, uninterested.

"Then you know the second grade is making gifts for fathers?" she asked bubbling with enthusiasm.

"Yes," I answered curtly.

"Well, I could use some help. Could you call about ten mothers and remind them of the project, and encourage them to participate?"

All of me silently screamed "no." I hadn't even liked the idea of a Christmas store at school. Our children are too spoiled now, I had thought. And schools don't even remember what Christmas is all about anyway. I hadn't planned to contribute anything to the project.

That's why I was surprised when I answered, "Of course."

"Oh, thank you," the relief was evident in her voice. She began calling out names and numbers. As I wrote, I thought, this is ridiculous. I've learned to say no. Why am I doing this?

We made polite conversation and I hung up confused. Now I would almost have to contribute something. I was officially involved with the program.

Sit down and talk to me about this, the silent voice urged.

"About this, Lord?"

Yes.

"I'll just stand here at the stove and confess my ugly attitude while I scrape eggs off the burner."

No, go upstairs and sit in your chair where you often talk to me.

Mostly because I didn't want to clean scrambled eggs off the stove, I went upstairs, plopped down in the old chair and without a moment's hesitation began, "Lord, I'm sorry about my ugly attitude. I'm usually willing to do my part. But I don't like this idea. Not many people will be thinking about you at a Christmas store. That's not fair. It's your birthday."

You could remind them.

"You mean just stand around and mumble, 'Do you know whose birthday it is?'"

Certainly not. That wouldn't glorify me at all.

"I know, Lord. I'm sorry. I just don't want to make anything and I don't want to go or call those people."

I want you to make something special.

"Me? What?"

Pencil holders.

"That's a good idea. That would be a good selling item for children to get for their fathers. What could I make them from?"

Orange juice cans. Start saving them now. You have over two months.

"What will I cover them with?"

You will paint them white and then paint a manger scene on them. You will use Scripture, 'For God so loved the world . . .' John 3:16"

"Oh, Lord, what a beautiful idea! I can't believe I'm

talking to you about orange juice cans, of all things. You really do care about little things. I had almost forgotten. I love your idea. I feel a little bit like Noah."

I went back downstairs to clean the stove and continued talking. "Lord, this is such a perfect gift for me to be making. I've always loved to walk into a business office and see a little handmade pencil holder sitting on a man's desk. Thank you for this idea, Lord. I didn't even want to be a part of this whole project, now I can hardly wait to get started." I opened my first can of orange juice and plopped the empty, washed can into a paper sack and put it in the pantry.

As I called the mothers on my list, everyone I talked with asked, "What are you going to make?"

I said, "I'm going to make pencil holders from orange juice cans and paint Baby Jesus in the manger on them and use Scripture."

Reactions were varied.

"Oh, I hope my daughter gets her daddy one."

Silence.

"What a lovely idea."

"I wish I could think of something."

"I really don't have time to make anything."

"Why don't you paint Santa Claus on them?"

I was so anxious to get ten large orange juice cans that my family asked, "What's with all the o.j.? You on some kind of health kick?"

I began making sketches of Baby Jesus. As I sketched one day I confessed to the Lord, "I really had bad feelings toward everyone who thought the store was a good idea. I was a spiritual snob, wasn't I?"

Yes.

Someone who knew I was making pencil holders suggested, "Why don't you put a new pencil in each one?"

Terrific, I thought. Once again a powerful suggestion

popped into my mind. *Get a pencil that tells about me.*

And so I bought ten pencils with the sign of the fish on them. Lettered in red was, "Jesus Christ, God's Son, Savior."

I stood back admiring the finished cans that sat on my dining room table.

One more thing.

"Yes, Lord?"

Love the people at the store who don't know me and may not appreciate your orange juice cans with my Son on them.

"You can see right into my heart, can't you. Sometimes I forget that. Please help me love those people."

I will. Just don't try to do it on your own.

29
The Old, Chipped Cup

A burden swelled inside my heart. As I prayed, I thought, it hurts, like a physical pain. God must stop this hurting. It musn't continue.

All night, though, the pain of the problem continued. I barely reached the fringes of sleep. Each time I nearly went to sleep, my mind sent an urgent message to my heart, "you have this burden." Then I was wide awake again, pleading with God for relief. Where was the peace that passed all understanding?

Finally, I stopped trying to escape into the world of sleep. With eyes opened wide I stared out the window at the stars. Toward morning my weary body and burning eyes screamed silently for rest, but my mind kept relaying the same frantic message—"remember your problem."

To my relief, the sky turned a quiet gray. Soon it would be time to get up and things would seem more normal as I moved about, engaged in activity.

As the first hint of pale pink crept across the heavens, I got up and slipped down to the kitchen. A cup of coffee would help. Something with no trace of God in it. I was tired of praying and believing. I wanted to forget about God for a while. He seemed to have forgotten about me.

But sitting at my kitchen table with the cup of steaming coffee, I began crying. Where was God? "Lord, I've called out to you all night and I've prayed every way I know how. I'm still confused, hurt. Haven't you heard me? Why must I suffer?"

I whispered aloud, "You have to give me some kind of an answer. I'll accept anything, even unchanged circumstances, as long as I know you're speaking to me. Just let me know you care. My faith is so small this morning and I don't understand suffering. All the books I've read aren't any help now. The Scriptures I can quote somehow aren't the answer right now. Help me. Maybe the Christian life isn't so real, after all."

Sobbing, I waited. I didn't expect a vision or anything like that, but I fully anticipated that God would speak to me someway and I intended to wait for him.

The sun slipped over the horizon and sent a few rays of sudden light through the window. It slanted across the kitchen sink and seemed to lay on our old wooden kitchen table, revealing its coarse grain. The light stopped at my coffee cup and I looked down at it.

It was an old, chipped cup. A friend had given me a set four years ago. They were all chipped now, but I could never bring myself to throw them away. They reminded me of the friend I hadn't seen in years and I loved the pattern of the cups. They were of the nostalgic, quaint, little girl carrying a box of salt under her arm and holding an umbrella over her head as the rain poured down. The child appeared unaware that the salt streamed out of the box—even in the rain. The old familiar words on the cup blurred through my tears.

I mistakenly read, "When it rains he pours."

Suddenly, I laughed out loud, covering my mouth with my hand to keep from waking others in the house. Joy sprang up in my heart and nodding my head I prayed, "Got'cha, Lord," feeling wonderfully comfortable with the short, almost slang prayer.

Marveling over the simple answer he'd given me, I let my mind form the words slowly. "It's during life's storms that God is able to pour out his love on us in a special way."

I made a firm decision. If God wanted to get my attention through my suffering in this particular storm so that he could bless me with his unspeakable love—then so be it.

I accepted the problem and the suffering almost with joy, thanking him with enthusiasm and praise and receiving his love. I have never felt quite as dependent on him as the morning he answered my plea through that old salt advertisement on a chipped cup.

As the sun filled my kitchen, and I heard my family getting up, it hardly seemed real that a few moments ago I had doubted his love for me.

30
Beyond the Blackberry Patch

As a child I often observed women confidently mothering their brood, knowing exactly what to buy in the grocery store, or driving with complete assurance to a destination, with a car full of squealing children.

And I told myself, someday I'll be doing that. I'll be all grown-up, married, and have children. But in my mind's eye, I wondered, how can that ever be? For it seemed I would always be a skinny, shy little girl merely peeking into the awesome world of adulthood.

I used to reason, I can't just stay a child—no one ever does. Growing up must happen sometime. But I can't imagine being one of them—an adult. I can't believe I'll do grown-up things like drinking coffee or sitting around and being still for hours or wanting to take a nap. And I can't believe I'll ever put cold cream on my face. I don't know how to be a mother—and who will ever love me and want me for his wife?

I tried not to think about the future too much, because deep down it frightened me terribly. I didn't like changes. I wanted to hold onto my childhood. I knew I would be content for the rest of my life to continue picking blackberries with the hot sun beating down on my back in the summer and marveling over seeing my own breath before me in the winter.

Zooming down a hill on skates, playing "kick-the-can," till the stars came out, sleeping late, reading all day if I wanted to, going to camp, feeding stray animals, rescuing drowning bugs, carefully cutting out a new book of paper dolls, and smiling to myself in a dark theater over Gene Autry's goodness, was the only life I knew.

I couldn't possibly see how I would give all this up in exchange for methodical grocery shopping, talking politely to other grown ladies, having permanents, and struggling with a child who had temper tantrums in the dime store.

As a teenager I occasionally thought about the future, getting married, and having children. But I decided that the future must be a long way off, because inside I still felt like a child.

When I went away to college, if I had had to choose sides, I would have quickly said I belonged with the children of the world rather than the adults.

In my early twenties I loved someone who loved me, and we began talking about marriage. The future I had imagined for so long was near—and yet, it didn't seem too different from yesterday.

The other evening I sat on my front steps and watched the sun disappear. The delicious coolness of the twilight touched me as the heat of the day faded away. Supper was over; the kitchen clean. I had even done some extra house cleaning and felt especially good about it.

I watched my husband move the sprinkler. We had just reseeded the front lawn. (Funny, as a child, I had taken grass for granted.)

Our thirteen-year-old daughter sprinted across the street to her best friend's house. She leaned impatiently against the door and waited for it to be opened, confident that she would be welcomed inside.

Our eight-year-old twin sons, engaged in a ball game across the street, would complain loudly when I called them in for a bath. (Maybe tonight, I would say yes when they begged for ten more minutes.)

Our sixteen-year-old daughter smiled slightly and waved good-bye to me from her boyfriend's car as they headed for the skating rink. (Could skating at a sophisticated rink, to the latest music, possibly be more fun than gliding on your skates down a sidewalk full of cracks that you could jump over?)

My cat rubbed, contentedly, against my knee. Looking down, I noticed some new touch-me-nots had come up by the steps. So many more than last year. A neighbor waved from across the street and I waved back enthusiastically.

Then just for a few moments, I saw my world and family as though they were a uniquely woven tapestry that I hadn't realized was of such dear workmanship—or so nearly completed. I marveled at each child and at my husband, bent over the sprinkler.

Contentment surged through me.

Suddenly, I became aware of the presence of God and he seemed to say to me, *Remember when you couldn't understand how all of this would happen? When you were even afraid of it and wanted to turn back? Remember when this very moment was in the faraway future and you were a little girl sitting up in a tree, afraid—wondering how it would ever really happen?*

"Yes, yes, Lord," I almost shouted. "I remember." (He knew about that day in the chinaberry tree!) Now my childhood seems as incredible and as faraway as the future once did.

Somehow, I've entered this impossible world of grown-ups. I'm really here, and yet, I'm not aware of ever having let go of my childhood. My devotion to Gene Autry and paper dolls hasn't completely faded. I still like to skate and feed stray animals. I love to pick blackberries—and now I can whip up a cobbler with them. Being a child isn't very different from becoming an adult. I never knew that until this moment. Crossing over wasn't frightening or even definite. I don't know when it happened!

I laughed softly to myself and my cat looked up at me wide-eyed. Surely, by now I've crossed over. My fortieth birthday had just passed.

And then I became aware of a startling thought, so profound that my heart beat rapidly and tears stung my eyes. *Someday, you'll leave this world and enter into my everlasting Kingdom. There's no need to be anxious now or try to figure it out. You can't. But it will happen just as surely and gently as you've moved from that world of childhood into the world of adults. My child, you can't imagine how wonderful it's going to be!*

PART SIX—THE CROSS

No one can kill me without my consent—I lay down my life voluntarily (John 10:18, TLB).

31
He Could Have Turned Back

I had never given much deep thought to Calvary—the cross. Oh, I wore a small, gold cross necklace, and occasionally I glanced up at the top of a church and thought that the cross looked pretty with the blue sky and fluffy clouds in the background.

And on Easter, the preacher was sure to talk about it. I tried to listen intently, but my mind wandered as I looked about the church at people, their clothes, and who was sitting with whom. And very carefully, in my mind, I surrounded the cross with Easter lilies and dogwood blooms to make it pleasant. I somehow managed to jump over the ugliness like a child playing hopscotch. "I can't possibly understand it, or do anything about it, so why think about it?" I decided flatly.

Most of the time I didn't think about the cross at all.

Then in my teens I saw a religious movie and in it they showed the crucifixion. Probably many things in the movie were not scriptural. To my knowledge, it wasn't made by Christians. But I slid way down in my seat when they came to the scene about the cross. There were no lilies or dogwood blooms. My heart beat wildly, and I wanted to get up and sit out in the lobby until it was over. But I couldn't seem to move. So I just sat there. Only I couldn't tell myself, this isn't real. It never happened. The spikes, the blood, the dull pounding, the heaviness of the cross with its splintered wood—they were a far cry from the little golden cross I sometimes wore, if it matched what I was wearing. Hurry, hurry, I thought, get through with this scene. But the cameras lingered on the details. I stared into the faces covered with evil laughter of those performing the execution. I was unable to convince myself, it's only a movie.

Finally, they stood the cross up with Jesus on it and I thought, it's over—at last. Now we'll see the resurrection. But still the cameras showed the cross. They zoomed in for a close-up of his face, hands, and feet. I looked away, but then looked back slowly at that face. In his eyes there wasn't as much pain as love and forgiveness for those he looked down upon.

The soldiers laughed and gambled for his robe. People milled around, some of them unconcerned. Children played. Those who loved Jesus agonized and cried, "Oh, why can't he die? Let him die! Why must he suffer so?" They hid their faces and moaned.

I was one of them now. Please, please, please don't show anymore, I cried in the darkness.

Then the scene was over. But it had been stamped permanently in my mind. Walking home slowly as I had done many Saturdays before, with the taste of popcorn in my mouth and the sun shining down on me, I thought, it was really that ugly, or worse. How had I for so long thought that it was somehow quick and not so bad, after all?

If only he could have been spared that suffering, I pondered. If only . . . .

I was an adult and the mother of four children when I learned, through Bible study and in Christian sharing groups, that Jesus didn't have to go to the cross. Billy Graham drove home that powerful thought in one of his sermons. He said that ten thousand legions of angels stood ready with swords drawn to rescue Jesus—if only he had let them.

I had come to grips with the fact that the cross had been agony for Jesus, and I had also recently, finally come to understand that he did it for *me* personally. But this new truth that he didn't have to be crucified was revolutionary!

He didn't want to die—not that horrible death, but he chose to. That's why he labored in prayer in the garden of Gethsemane. That's why he asked God to let the cup pass from him. He recoiled from sin and all it represented. He didn't want to suffer and die physically when he could have just zoomed up to heaven without pain, humiliation, or isolation.

But more than anything, he wanted his Father's will— glory to God—to come out of an ugly situation. He wanted to lay down his life that I might live, after death; and now might live abundantly each day of my life. And he was willing for God to make him willing to die.

Jesus went like a lamb to slaughter, and sinful man obtained a reprieve—if he chose to accept it. There's always the choice.

Just recently in a Bible study someone said, in a voice barely audible, "You know how the Vietnamese tortured our men. Well, think how much more Romans enjoyed torturing a Jew. In Isaiah it tells that they even pulled out his beard."

Someone added, "People who were crucified often died of suffocation. They had to push up with their feet to get each breath. Each time Jesus breathed, he had to push himself up to get air."

"It was so slow," someone said.

Another told how when a person was scourged that the whip, with bits of glass in it, pulled out the person's flesh.

"And they took off all his clothes. He hung there naked—almost like—a piece of meat—for me."

The teacher added softly, "Even so, the worst part—God turned away from him as he bore your sins and mine. God is so holy and pure that he cannot look upon sin. When Jesus accepted the cross, he also took upon himself every dirty, ugly, and perverse sin that ever had been or would be committed. The Father turned away. Jesus suffered the desolation of separation from God the Father. Jesus died for our sins.

He didn't have to do it! He didn't have to do it! I thought, wildly. He had a choice. He could have turned back at any time. Walking up the hill—even on the cross, he could have come down and said, "Enough of this." He remained all powerful.

Thank you, dear Jesus, for not turning back at the cross; for dying that horrible death for me; for taking my sins on your back. Thank you now that you want to live your life through me. Welcome into my heart. There'll be times when I'll want to turn back. Times when I'll forget about that cross you died on for me. Times when all I can think about is *me, me, me.* Help me not to turn back when those times come. You sure weren't a quitter. You moaned with love, "It is finished."

I have decided to follow Jesus,
No turning back, no turning back.
The world behind me, the cross before me,
No turning back, no turning back.
Though none go with me, still I will follow.
No turning back,
No turning back.

Acknowledgments

Chapter 3 "The Football and I"
From *Home Life*, January 1975.
© Copyright 1974 The Sunday
School Board of the Southern
Baptist Convention. All rights
reserved. Used by permission.

Chapter 12 "A Little Bit of Light"
Copyright © 1977, Scripture Press
Publications, Inc., Wheaton, Ill.
60187. Reprinted by permission
from *Power for Living*.

Chapter 13 "Peppermint Miracle"
© 1976, SP Publications, Inc.
World rights reserved. Used by
permission.

Chapter 20 "Season of Courage"
Reprinted from *Sunday Digest*,
© 1976, David C. Cook Publishing Co.,
Elgin, IL Used by permission.

Chapter 21 "Something Special for Angela"
Reprinted by permission from
Guideposts Magazine, Copyright ©
1975 by Guideposts Associates, Inc.,
Carmel, New York 10512.